managing
RESOURCES

instant manager
skills for success

managing
RESOURCES

BERNICE WALMSLEY

HODDER
EDUCATION
PART OF HACHETTE LIVRE UK

The publisher has used its best endeavours to ensure that the URLs for external websites referred to in this book are correct and active at the time of going to press. However, the publisher and the author have no responsibility for the websites and can make no guarantee that a site will remain live or that the content will remain relevant, decent or appropriate.

Orders: Please contact Bookpoint Ltd, 130 Milton Park, Abingdon, Oxon OX14 4SB. Telephone: (44) 01235 827720, Fax: (44) 01235 400454. Lines are open from 9.00 to 5.00, Monday to Saturday, with a 24-hour message answering service. You can also order through our website www.hoddereducation.co.uk.

British Library Cataloguing in Publication Data
A catalogue record for this title is available from the British Library.

ISBN-13: 978 0340 947371

First published   2010
Impression number   10 9 8 7 6 5 4 3 2 1
Year   2013 2012 2011 2010

Copyright © 2010 Bernice Walmsley

Cover image © Brian Hagiwara/FoodPix/Getty Images
Photographer [logo] – Niki Sianni

Typeset by Transet Limited, Coventry, England.
Printed in Great Britain for Hodder Education, an Hachette Livre UK Company, 338 Euston Road, London NW1 3BH, by Cox & Wyman, Reading, Berkshire RG1 8EX.

Hachette Livre UK's policy is to use papers that are natural, renewable and recyclable products and made from wood grown in sustainable forests. The logging and manufacturing processes are expected to conform to the environmental regulations of the country of origin.

The Chartered Management Institute

CMI

The Chartered Management Institute is the only chartered professional body that is dedicated to management and leadership. We are committed to raising the performance of business by championing management.

We represent 86,000 individual managers and have 450 corporate members. Within the Institute there are also a number of distinct specialisms, including the Institute of Business Consulting and Women in Management Network.

We exist to help managers tackle the management challenges they face on a daily basis by raising the standard of management in the UK. We are here to help individuals become better managers and companies develop better managers.

We do this through a wide range of products and services, from practical management checklists to tailored training and qualifications. We produce research on the latest 'hot' management issues, provide a vast array of useful information through our online management information centre, as well as offering consultancy services and career information.

You can access these resources 'off the shelf' or we can provide solutions just for you. Our range of products and services is designed to ensure organisations and managers develop their potential and excel. Whether you are at the start of your career or a proven performer in the boardroom, we have something for you.

We engage policy makers and opinion formers and, as the leading authority on management, we are regularly consulted on a range of management issues. Through our in-depth research and regular policy surveys of members, we have a deep understanding of the latest management trends.

For more information visit our website **www.managers.org.uk** or call us on **01536 207307**.

Chartered Manager

Transform the way you work

The Chartered Management Institute's Chartered Manager award is the ultimate accolade for practising professional managers. Designed to transform the way you think about your work and how you add value to your organisation, it is based on demonstrating measurable impact.

This unique award proves your ability to make a real difference in the workplace.

Chartered Manager focuses on the six vital business skills of:

- Leading people
- Managing change
- Meeting customer needs
- Managing information and knowledge
- Managing activities and resources
- Managing yourself

Transform your organisation

There is a clear and well-established link between good management and improved organisational performance. Recognising this, the Chartered Manager scheme requires individuals to demonstrate how they are applying their leadership and change management skills to make significant impact within their organisation.

Transform your career

Whatever career stage a manager is at Chartered Manager will set them apart. Chartered Manager has proven to be a stimulus to career progression, either via recognition by their current employer or through the motivation to move on to more challenging roles with new employers.

But don't take just our word for it ...
Chartered Manager has transformed the careers and organisations of managers in all sectors.

- *'Being a Chartered Manager was one of the main contributing factors which led to my recent promotion.'*
  Lloyd Ross, Programme Delivery Manager, British Nuclear Fuels

- *'I am quite sure that a part of the reason for my success in achieving my appointment was due to my Chartered Manager award which provided excellent, independent evidence that I was a high quality manager.'*
  Donaree Marshall, Head of Programme Management Office, Water Service, Belfast

- *'The whole process has been very positive, giving me confidence in my strengths as a manager but also helping me to identify the areas of my skills that I want to develop. I am delighted and proud to have the accolade of Chartered Manager.'*
  Allen Hudson, School Support Services Manager, Dudley Metropolitan County Council

- *'As we are in a time of profound change, I believe that I have, as a result of my change management skills, been able to provide leadership to my staff. Indeed, I took over three teams and carefully built an integrated team, which is beginning to perform really well. I believe that the process I went through to gain Chartered Manager status assisted me in achieving this and consequently was of considerable benefit to my organisation.'*
  George Smart, SPO and D/Head of Resettlement, HM Prison Swaleside

To find out more or to request further information please visit our website **www.managers.org.uk/cmgr** or call us on **01536 207429**.

Contents

CHAPTER 03

CHAPTER 04

CHAPTER 05

CHAPTER 06

CHAPTER 07

CHAPTER 08

CHAPTER 09

CHAPTER 10

CHAPTER 11

CHAPTER 12

Foreword

There has never been a greater need for better management and leadership skills in the UK. As we've seen over the past couple of years, it's all too often the case that management incompetence takes the blame for high-profile, costly and sometimes tragic failures. Put this in the context of a world dominated by changing technology and growing international competition, and every manager in this country has a responsibility for ensuring that he or she has the best possible skills to contribute to successful business performance.

So it is alarming that just one in five managers in the UK are professionally qualified. The truth is that we spend less on management development in the UK than our European competitors. Effectively this means that, if you want to develop professionally, if you want to boost your career chances, or if you just want recognition for the work you do, the onus is on you – the individual – to improve your skills. What it also means is that all of us – individual managers, employers and policy makers – need to answer difficult questions about how well equipped we are to lead in the twenty-first century. Are our standards slipping? How capable are we when it comes to meeting the skill requirements of modern business? Studies show that project management, alliance-building and communication skills are the three key 'over-arching' skills that must be mastered by the successful manager. But how many people can honestly claim they have mastery over all three?

In recent years the news has been dominated by stories focusing on breathtaking management failures. The collapse of the banking sector has been much-analysed and will continue to be discussed in the years to come. It's not just the private sector. Vast amounts of column inches have been devoted to investigations of failures across the health and social care sector, too. The spotlight has also been on management, at an individual level, as the recession deepened in the aftermath of the banking crisis, with dramatic rises in the UK's unemployment levels. Many managers are fighting an ongoing battle to control costs and survive with reduced credit and slowing demand. They are also struggling to prove their worth, to show they meet required standards now, and in the long-term.

But imagine a world where management and leadership enables top-class performance right across British businesses, the public sector and our not-for-profit organisations – where management isn't a byword for bureaucracy and failure, but plays a real role in boosting performance. The way to achieve such a realistic utopia is by developing the skills that will help you, as a manager, perform to the best of your capability. And that is why this book will help. Its aim is to provide you with practical, digestible advice that you can take straight from the pages to apply in your working environment.

Does any of this matter? Well, you wouldn't want your accounts signed off by someone lacking a financial qualification. You certainly wouldn't let an unqualified surgeon anywhere near you with a scalpel, nor would you seek an unqualified lawyer to represent your interests. Why, then, should your employer settle for management capability that is second best? It means that you need to take time out to develop your skills so that these can be evaluated and so you can stand out from the competition.

What's more, managers will play a critical role in determining how well the UK meets a wide range of challenges over the next decade. How can managers foster innovation to promote economic growth? How do they tackle the gender pay gap and the continued under-representation of women in the boardroom, as part of building truly fair, diverse organisations? Managers in all sectors will need to learn how to lead their teams through the changes we face; they will also need to be able to manage change. Above all, managers will need to grasp the nettle when it comes to managing information and knowledge. The key will rest in how they learn to manage themselves.

First-class management and leadership really can drive up both personal and corporate performance. It can boost national productivity and enhance social wellbeing. If you want to be the best manager you can be, this book is for you. In one go it will provide you with practical advice and the experience of business leaders. It is also a fascinating and enthralling read!

Ruth Spellman OBE
Chief Executive
Chartered Management Institute

01

Introduction

Who should read this book?

If you want to upgrade your management skills, then this series of books – part of the Instant Manager series – is for you. The series covers a range of skills needed by today's managers including those set out in the employer-led set of standards (the National Occupational Standards) for leadership and management drawn up to improve the productivity and profitability of organisations in the UK. These standards are also aimed at helping with career development so are of benefit to employees and employers alike.

This book is for any manager – new or experienced – who needs help with managing the resources they have at their disposal. It is not jargon-filled or too complicated and theory-bound. It contains practical advice to help you in your working life. So, if you need to acquire the knowledge needed to make sure that you make the best use of resources such as finances, knowledge, technology, suppliers and your team in order to do your job effectively then this book will help you to acquire the necessary skills. These skills will be useful to managers of all sorts of organisations, whether large or small, run for profit or non-profit, including companies, charities and government departments.

A range of topics, linked by the common themes of understanding and enhancing your own skills set in relation to your work role, will be covered in each book in the series in the form of ten questions on the topic, plus an interview with a well-known business expert. In this book you will find the answers to questions that will show you how to manage activities and resources.

At the end of each chapter, after a specific question has been answered, there will be a summary of the chapter and a short action checklist, which will give you a series of practical steps you will need to take to overcome the challenge of that aspect of using and managing activities and resources.

The skills that you will learn in this book are vital to your success as a manager. Of course, the skills you need are many and varied, so in this book we will be concentrating on the ones you need to manage resources – budgets and finance, technology, physical resources such as equipment, materials and premises, knowledge and information and suppliers while ensuring Health and Safety requirements are met, managing the impact on the environment, making decisions and supporting team and virtual working.

What skills do you need to manage resources?

Many of the skills necessary to manage resources are those that all managers will need – the general skills that you will use every day. But all managers need to solve a range of problems and manage a different blend of resources in their organisations and there is a wide range of specific skills that will be vital if you are to ensure that all the resources at your disposal are put to best use for your organisation.

General management skills such as involving others and communication will be vital when you are supporting team working for example, and more specific ones such as risk management will be vital in assessing the impact your work has on the environment or dealing with health and safety matters, while the skills of negotiating and strategic thinking will be essential when selecting and dealing with suppliers. In any management role decision making will be necessary but when dealing with complex activities and resources this skill is especially important.

Let's look in a little more detail at the skills that will be necessary to manage resources successfully:

● **Decision making** – most management tasks involve an element of decision making but in using and managing resources there are many complex decisions to be made. These decisions must be made in a structured way and the process of decision making is dealt with in Chapter 7.
● **Thinking strategically** – the ability to think strategically is needed in order to solve complex problems and then to use resources efficiently and effectively. This skill is especially useful when assessing the need for additional finance or dealing with suppliers. It is invaluable when planning how resources of all types can best be used in the business.
● **Risk management** – this skill will be used in many areas but is essential when dealing with health and safety matters or in making financial decisions. It involves identifying the probability and effect of problems occurring, and then minimising the impact of the effect of those occurrences on the business.
● **Information management** – understanding the knowledge and information that exists in an organisation and then ensuring that it is used and shared to maximise the benefit to the business is essential in virtually all organisations. It is also necessary to protect information

from use that is not authorised. This skill is dealt with specifically in Chapter 8.

- **Contingency planning** – when making decisions it is important to consider what could go wrong and then to make plans to deal with that situation. This is contingency planning and it is an essential skill in any decision-making process that uses physical resources.
- **Negotiating** – this is a skill involving getting the best deal for your organisation that will come to the fore when dealing with suppliers and is dealt with in detail in Chapter 10. In any negotiations there is more to consider than merely the amount being paid so balancing a diverse range of criteria and requirements is an important aspect of negotiating skills.

After that brief overview, let's move on to the challenges that will meet you in the first of our questions, which looks at a topic of prime importance to many managers – budgets and finance.

02

How can you manage a budget and arrange finance?

Managing the financial aspects of your work role is an important part of almost any manager's responsibilities, so becoming financially 'literate' is vital to your success. Managing a budget is central to this and, as always, results must be monitored if performance is to be improved and everything kept on track. Understanding how a budget can help in planning to get results and how different types of finance are useful in different situations will ensure that you give your plans for your area of responsibility the best chance of a positive outcome. Financial management is a skill that can be learned and improved. First, in this chapter about financial matters, we will look at the principles of preparing a budget that will serve its purpose and provide you with a good basis for controlling and improving performance.

Preparing a budget

First it will be useful to define just what a budget is – and what it isn't. A budget is part of your planning processes and will help you to achieve your objectives for the organisation or for your area of responsibility. It is not some sort of forecast of what will happen. It will not predict results – rather it will help you to achieve the results that you have planned, so you will need to be sure of the direction in which you want to take the organisation or your department and how you will get there before you start to prepare your budget. It will:

- ensure that you can afford your planned projects and ongoing operations
- help you to make financial decisions
- stay in control of the financial aspects of your job
- quantify your goals for your sales, your expenditure and your profits.

There are many benefits of preparing a budget to encompass and achieve all the plans that you have – or that have been decided by others in the management chain for your department – and these include:

- helping you to make the best use of the money available
- helping you to meet your objectives by giving you additional ways of ensuring that you keep on track
- ensuring that the correct amount of resources is allocated to each area and to each project
- keeping track of the performance of the project or business
- improving your decision-making processes by giving you the information you need and clarifying your ideas
- making plans for the future
- keeping track of your cash flow

- showing where costs can be reduced
- helping you to predict problems.

From the above it is obvious that preparing a comprehensive budget will bring many advantages and help you to be effective. So, how do you go about preparing a budget? The first step is to make sure that you have allowed sufficient time to do the job properly. A quick adding up of what you think you will have to spend in the coming financial period will not be sufficient – it must be a far more comprehensive exercise than that. Next you must be clear about your vision – where are you going and why? How are you going to get there? Next you will need to organise all the information you need to prepare your budget. There is a variety of areas that you will need to take into account and you will need to ask a lot of questions to arrive at the information about income and expenditure that will go into an effective budget. Ensure that you include the following:

Direct costs

These are the costs of the sales and will include materials and components, packaging, the cost of any sub-contracting and so on. It will be obvious which these costs are – the test is if the cost goes up the more you sell then the costs are direct.

Fixed costs

This will include costs such as salaries, rent, business rates, machinery and equipment, tax and national insurance, fuel, stationery, travel and transport/vehicles.

Sales forecasts

Next you need to look at what you expect to sell – i.e. your predicted revenue. It is vital that this figure is arrived at with full knowledge of the market conditions, plans for the future and previous sales figures where appropriate. It should be a realistic figure rather than an educated guess or a wish list. A forecast of sales is essential as, if you do not know how many of your product or how much of your service you are going to sell, you will not be able to calculate costs and the budget will not then be as useful.

When preparing a budget it is usually necessary, and indeed desirable, to involve other people in all but the smallest of businesses and even then it is likely that the business's accountant will have to be involved in terms of supplying details of expenditure and also advice. If others in the organisation have responsibility for aspects of expenditure or revenue then they should have input to the budget. This will not only make the task easier and a more accurate result possible but it will also ensure that staff feel involved and remain motivated. Promoting ownership of the budget in this way will make it much more likely that there will be a commitment to meeting it.

Another way in which others will be involved in a budget is in the final stages when it may be necessary to present the figures to someone else for approval. This may be an immediate superior in the case of where the budget is for a department or other part of the organisation. It may be that not all of the ideas and proposals contained in the budget meet with approval or more explanation is required. In this case it is advisable to be prepared to negotiate and explain the budget by deciding in advance the areas where some negotiation is possible without compromising the main aims and having all the necessary information to hand.

When preparing a budget the figures should be put together with future reviews in mind. It should be easy to measure performance against the budget so this preparation stage is the ideal time to ensure that the necessary information is collected during the accounting period. In the next section we will look at how performance against budget can be measured.

INSTANT TIP

Take note when preparing your budget of the level of sales at which you reach the break-even point. i.e. the amount you need to sell to cover your costs. If you're not sure you can reach this point then the organisation is in difficulty and corrective action will be essential.

Monitoring performance against your budget

There are a number of ways in which a well-prepared budget can help to make a manager more aware of how the business is progressing towards its aims. You will be able to:

- Note where more (or less) has been spent than had been planned. This will obviously prompt an investigation at some level to ascertain whether or not the expenditure was justified. Find out if the budget was wrong or if the objectives have changed, for instance.
- See where revenues have decreased or increased. It is important to see the reasons behind such changes so that problems or mistakes can be corrected or, in the case of increased revenues, more of the same can be done.
- Plan cash flow.

So, how can you measure your performance against your budget? First, you will need to be sure you are comparing like with like. This can be made easier, as we said earlier, by compiling the budget with monitoring in mind. If you are going to change how a figure is used in budget setting (for example, the way revenues are calculated or costs per unit of product or service) then you should have a good reason for doing so. You will need to make sure that you are aware of any such changes and of the effect they will have on your calculations when monitoring performance against the projected figures. There is little point in comparing figures whose method of calculation has changed from the way they were used in setting the budget to a different way when the actual figures are compiled. When you have checked this you can consider how the actual figures you have achieved compare with the projected figures in your budget. Have you achieved your sales forecasts? Were your forecasts of costs – both fixed and variable – accurate? And if not, why not? This is your opportunity to see how you are doing and to work out how you can improve. As always, if you find something is going wrong then you must take corrective action. Look at each of the areas in turn.

Income

If your actual income is below the figure you have budgeted for then an analysis of just why this has happened will be necessary. Have you sold fewer products than forecast? If so, you will need to check why. This could be for a variety of reasons such as:

- Problems in the market generally – in times of economic downturn then sales volumes may fall.
- Poor performance by sales staff – do you need more staff, fewer or just different, more effective ones? Or maybe some training is required?

- Changes in demand for your particular product – if you are in tune with your market then you should be able to predict when certain products will be subject to reduced demand. Fashions change but if you are in a volatile market then you need a contingency plan to deal with these changes. Good market knowledge and a proactive approach will ensure that you introduce new products in a timely way so that the natural lifespan of a product in sales terms will not be overlooked.
- Incorrect forecasts – was the reasoning behind a particular sales figure flawed? Your projected figures may be too high or too low and both will have an effect on how you deal with costs and so on. You will need to investigate to get sufficient information to take corrective action.
- At this point you should also check the timing of sales. Did your income each month match what you had predicted or were some months busier or quieter than expected? Are you getting paid quickly enough for the goods or services you have supplied? This will have an obvious effect on the cash flow of the business so is of particular importance. If you find that the number of debtor days (the number of days that, on average, your customers have taken to pay for what you have supplied) has increased then you will need to look carefully at your credit control procedures.

If you find that the quantity of sales has not fallen then the problem – unless a mistake has been made in the compilation of the figures – will be that the average price obtained for the goods or services has fallen. Again, there may be a variety of reasons for this but a close examination of the prices being achieved will show where the problem is. It will be necessary to check:

- By product area – is one product or service in particular pulling down the results?
- By sales area – are the expected prices being achieved by some sales people and not by others?
- Large orders – exceptionally large orders can skew the figures and, while a volume discount is often necessary to obtain such orders, the overall profitability must be maintained.
- The market – are prices generally depressed? How is the competition faring?

Again prompt corrective action will be necessary once the root of the problem has been exposed.

Expenditure

Keeping track of what you have actually spent compared with what you planned to spend is often an illuminating process. It is necessary to go through the expenditure under each budget heading. This will highlight the following:

- Changes in fixed costs – have you had a rent increase that you did not expect? Or maybe you have employed a key member of staff at a higher rate of pay than you had budgeted?
- How variable costs have changed in response to increases or decreases in sales. You may find, for instance, that a fall in the volume of sales results in a corresponding decrease in material costs. You should check that the decrease is the amount you would have expected, i.e. in line with your costing for that product.
- Where the timing of outgoings have changed. This could be as a result of changes in how and when you pay your suppliers and will affect your cash flow.

INSTANT TIP

Set a specific time – the first week of each month for example – when you will compare actual income and expenditure with your forecasted figures on a regular basis. This will avoid any problem going unnoticed for too long. If you discover large differences, find out why they have occurred and take action immediately.

When monitoring performance in this way it is also a good idea to compare budgets year on year. In particular, look at:

● Sales – comparing actual sales this year with actual sales in previous years is a good way to see if the measures to improve that you have taken in the past are proving successful.
● Costs – are they increasing or decreasing?
● Profits – most organisations (with the exception of charities and non-profit organisations) are in business to make a profit. If you do not increase profits year on year then you should be actively searching for ways in which you can make this happen.

Having identified the cause of the budget variances, corrective action must then be taken to solve the problems. This will require discussion and negotiation with the people involved in that area of the organisation and also may need budget revision which will often require agreement from senior management. The corrective action that is necessary will, of course, depend on the nature of the problem that is uncovered but may include:

● Resolving the issue that caused a fall in sales – this may be to make changes to sales methods or personnel, to the prices being charged or to the actual products or services on offer.

● Where possible, renegotiating prices paid for supplies or reducing the amounts being purchased.

● Budget revision if the problem cannot be resolved so that the sales or expenditure forecasts can be brought back on track.

● Learning the lessons from the variances discovered so that budgets for the next period are adjusted accordingly.

The information that is produced when monitoring performance against a set budget is invaluable. The best way to improve is to be clear about what is currently happening and then to analyse any deviations from the budget. You will find out what is going wrong and what is being done right. Management decisions can only be made if managers are in possession of complete information. A budget can be the basis for this and the analysis that comes from the monitoring process will provide the necessary detail.

Case study

When initially establishing the business, the owner of a small publishing operation was asked by his bank to provide a budget for his first year of business. He found this to be such a useful exercise that he continued to prepare a budget every year. He found that it helped him not only to control expenditure but also greatly increased his understanding of the business. He started the annual reviews two to three months before the year end of each year to give himself plenty of time to look at all the options that he was considering for his business in the coming year. Having the figures available in detail allowed him to see just where his profit would be coming from and to increase or decrease sales efforts and marketing for specific product areas accordingly.

After three years of operation he decided to take his annual budgeting process a step further and initiated monthly reviews of income and expenditure. He conducted these reviews as soon as he received the monthly figures from his accounts manager. He involved this accounts manager plus his sales manager in these reviews. Being able to take action as soon as a problem was spotted gave the owner and his managers the confidence to develop the business while still feeling secure that they were keeping within their financial limits. So, for example, if he spotted an area of sales that was underperforming he would increase advertising or alternatively he may have decided to discontinue a product or increase prices to resolve the problem and bring the budget back on track.

He commented, 'Having this control gave me the confidence to grow the business with the knowledge that I was not taking undue risks. I can see early on in the process the effect that an increase in sales to a new market, for example, would have on my costs, so decisions to develop the business were easy to take. We've doubled our turnover in the last four years.'

INSTANT TIP

It is important to be aware that the monitoring of budgets may uncover incidences of fraud. In this case it will be necessary to report the details to senior management and/or the appropriate authorities.

Managing finance to achieve objectives

By keeping a close check on how areas of the business are performing against set financial forecasts, it will be possible to make changes along the way so that objectives are met. The areas that should be checked on a regular basis include sales, cash flow and expenditure.

Sales

If sales levels are not as high as forecast it will be necessary to find out why as soon as possible and then to take remedial action. For example, you may need to recalculate unit costs and sell at a different price to ensure that costs are covered while making sales more attractive to your potential customers or it may be necessary to increase advertising to support marketing efforts to sell more. Sales need to be carefully managed to ensure that they are profitable. For example, while a large order may seem like the answer to a problem of lack of sales, if the extra investment in raw materials, additional staff and new machinery mean that an increased overdraft facility is necessary to meet it then it may mean that it causes more problems than it solves. These problems could include:

- Increased costs leading to low margins.
- A large order may distract everyone's attention from regular customers leading to a loss of routine orders.
- Poor cash flow if the new customer does not pay on time or demands longer payment terms or raw materials, etc., need to be paid for before the goods you produce are paid for and so on.

Whatever the reason for sales levels being lower than forecast, it is likely to have an impact on finances. If revenue is reduced or delayed then it will have an effect on the organisation's cash flow and this is dealt with next.

Cash flow

Well-managed cash flow is vital to the survival of any organisation. Cash flow is the amount of money going out of a business, detailing when and where it is going against the cash coming in – again detailing when and where from. A well-prepared cash flow forecast will ensure that the business has sufficient cash to meet its requirements without needing an unexpected – and usually expensive – overdraft. This can be a delicate balance to achieve and it is worth taking the time to plan the timing of income and expenditure very carefully so that financial problems do not derail the business. Apart from preparing a cash flow forecast that will highlight potential problem times there are several measures that can be taken to avoid cash flow becoming a problem. These include:

- Getting income into the business, i.e. getting your sales invoices paid on time, so that the necessary payments to your suppliers can be made, is essential. Credit control is therefore an important function in the management of cash flow.
- Managing credit control very closely. Having a routine of when and how payments are chased up is vital and it is always useful to know exactly what the position is. Measures such as keeping track of Debtor Days (how many days invoices are outstanding) and regular reviews will ensure the situation is kept under control.
- Debt factoring – arranging for another organisation to collect all your outstanding payments in exchange for a percentage of the amount outstanding.

- Invoice discounting – giving customers a small discount for prompt payment.
- Negotiate deals with suppliers to gain the maximum amount of time before a debt becomes due for payment. This is especially important in the case of regular supplies, although it is always preferable to reach a deal that keeps everyone – both you and your suppliers – satisfied that the deal is workable.
- Do not take on orders that you are unable to fulfil profitably at the price agreed.
- Reduce stock levels to ensure that not too much money is tied up in stock at any time.
- Planned borrowing is almost always cheaper than borrowing money to cover an emergency so use the cash flow forecast to help with this.

In short, the aim must be to get money into the business and keep it there for as long as possible. Accounting software is available to assist with the preparation of cash flow forecasts.

Expenditure

Again, a careful check must be kept on how much is being spent. If you have set a budget for items of expenditure and this budget is exceeded at any point, then you will have to find out why this has happened. It may be, for example, that a major supplier has increased prices so you will have to look at possible alternative suppliers. Or you may find that you have used more of an item – for example, fuel – than had been budgeted for. If too much of an item has been used in the production of items for sale it may be necessary to examine the design of that item to see if the raw materials content – and therefore the cost – can be reduced. If this is not possible then it may be necessary to increase the prices charged to customers to allow for the increased usage.

The objectives set for a business must be at the front of every manager's mind when making decisions that affect the finances of a business. Performance indicators should be set up that will show when an objective is not being met. In terms of financial measures, these could include:

- Cash flow – see the section above.
- Profitability – make sure that unplanned expenditure or lower prices do not decrease the organisation's sales margins.
- Debtor days – how long your debtors take to pay your invoices.
- Finance costs – setting a target for the amount to be paid in interest and other charges for the finance needed to run the business is important in that it will draw attention to what is often a major part of the budget and also will ensure that charges are not allowed to escalate.

In all cases where it becomes apparent that objectives are not on target to be met action must be taken to remedy the situation. This may be one or more of a range of actions including tightening up credit control, reducing costs and reviewing large orders for profitability.

INSTANT TIP

If you are not able to obtain payment from customers quickly enough to ensure good cash flow, consider using a factoring service. This is where a finance house will, in effect, 'buy' invoices at a discounted price from an organisation and then be responsible for collecting the payments for themselves.

Delegating responsibility for budgets

In all but the smallest organisations it will be necessary for work to be delegated on a regular basis and this includes the responsibility for budgets. However, for many managers delegation is something that can be difficult to do. Nevertheless it brings several advantages to an organisation including:

- Freeing up time for a senior manager to plan and oversee the business.
- Motivating the person to whom responsibilities are delegated – this applies only if the delegation is carried out in the right way. This means ensuring that the person being given the responsibility understands what is to be done and has all the tools and resources to do a good job.
- Making the best use of the abilities available in an individual or a team.
- Trust in senior management will be built up.

It is essential to delegate in the correct way. Resources must be made available to ensure success in the task being delegated. This can include training, ensuring that time to carry out the task is made available and the necessary support from management. Providing sufficient support – being available to discuss problems and give advice – while not over-supervising the job (this can mean that just as much time is taken up by the manager delegating the work) can be a difficult balance to achieve but will be worthwhile if it means more work getting done and improved performance is the result.

If someone has responsibility for an area of a business, for example, for production or sales, then they will need to be given a budget for income and expenditure within that area to ensure that objectives are met. The key to success in delegating responsibility for budgets is clear definition. Financial targets for all items of expenditure and income must be agreed by all parties in advance, as must any accepted variances from the agreed targets.

Making someone who reports to you responsible for a budget, i.e. delegating control of financial matters in a particular area, must be done with great care. As we said earlier in this section, it is essential that the person taking on the responsibility is given all the tools needed to do the job. This includes full involvement in the process of agreeing targets for their area of responsibility and a budget to do the job. Without this involvement at the earliest stage of planning, the employee may feel that the job – and its budget – is not really owned by them but belongs to 'management'. It may also engender a feeling of resentment. Neither of these things will lead to the best performance in the job and it is less likely that budgets will be adhered to. It is also important to include training where necessary and the facility to draw upon a senior colleague's expertise if needed.

Identifying the need for additional finance

Although the organisation may be generating some surplus income from current operations, this is often not sufficient for the financing of future plans. These plans could involve a move to bigger – or smaller – premises, investment in new machinery, research and development, entry into new markets, new product launches or an increase in production or supply capacity. In almost all cases where additional finances are required for future plans, the aim will be to maximise profits. It is therefore necessary to conduct a detailed examination into exactly why the finance is required, the amount needed and what the implications will be in terms of increased outgoings and increased income.

An essential part of this examination is the business plan. This will usually be able to show you not only how much extra finance is required but also when it will be needed and for exactly what purpose. As any form of borrowed finance will cost money in terms of interest payments and fees, it is essential that it is not borrowed until it is needed and this could mean that you will not need access to the finance until late in the planned project. You may need to agree availability with your lenders before commencing the project but then plan to take up the finance in stages to suit the project development and to minimise costs.

So, let's look at how the business plan can assist in deciding whether or not – and also when – finance will be required. A well-written business plan will include:

- An overview – this can be useful for the bank or other financial institutions considering finance for the organisation's plans as it will summarise the business plan and set out a brief résumé for the business. This may play a crucial part in a lender's decision-making process.
- The organisation's strategy – its vision, how it will grow and when, will be important in convincing any potential lender that the business is on the right track.
- The current state of the market in which the organisation operates – including details of the organisation's products and their place in the market, details of its customer base and its competitors.
- Financial forecasts including income and expenditure details, profit predictions, cash flow forecasts, details of assets and liabilities, sales forecasts and the funding required for planned projects. It should also include plans for repayment of any financing that may be needed and the security that may be available for loans. This section is extremely important – it contains the nuts and bolts that a financial institution will use to arrive at a decision on finance as it will inform them of the likelihood of the debt being repaid.

- Future development plans – this is where you can start to identify the need for additional finance. Quantifying the costs involved in future developments and the expected return on investment will make a case for the financial institution or other lender to consider.
- Personnel matters – how many people are employed, details of the qualifications, experience and standing of key people in the business, training plans and so on.
- A summary of how you do the work – i.e. what you do to make money and what machinery and information technology you use.

A business plan that covers all of these areas can be useful in both deciding where additional finance is needed and also in providing a case to present to possible providers of that finance. It will have set out the development plans for the business over the coming year, five years or other period covered by the business plan. Essentially, a business plan can be used to explain the business, along with its aims, visions and goals, to potential investors. It can make a case for why someone should invest in a business or lend money to it, showing what would be the benefits for both them and for the business. It is also useful to include plans and timescales regarding how the money will be paid back. If business plans are put together partly with the aim of securing additional finance (and partly for planning purposes, of course) they can be tailored to suit the prospective source of that finance. So, for example, if you're looking for equity investors or a loan from a bank, you will need to make clear how you intend to pay back the money or, in the case of shareholders, letting them have a detailed forecast about the share price performance, dividends and so on. The important thing is for the business plan to make a case for funding and to make the organisation, its management and its plans for the future an attractive proposition.

As we said earlier, finance can be needed in a variety of situations. It is almost always needed by start up businesses.

However, in an established business, additional finance needs may include:

- new products
- expanding production capacity
- new technology
- new markets
- new premises
- acquisitions and takeovers
- running costs.

New products

If an organisation is going to expand by widening its product base, or is going to maintain profitability by replacing products that have reached the end of their life cycles with new ones, then extra finance will usually be needed. Before the launch of a new product, and before any profit is possible from such products, there will be costs that will have to be financed. These include the research costs to produce a different product and also so that the organisation can conduct any research necessary to be sure that there is indeed a sufficiently high demand for the proposed product. It may be that prototypes will have to be produced and tested and that extensive market research including customer surveys will have to be carried out.

Expanding production capacity

If there is sufficient demand for a product then a business can make economies of scale by producing more of the same type of product. With a reduced unit cost, greater profits will be possible.

The equipment needed to facilitate this sort of expansion can include machinery, extensions to premises, new technology and tools and, as it can be extremely expensive, will need to be seen as a long-term investment in the organisation.

New technology

This may be used to expand production capacity as noted above but it can also be a way of making all types of systems – customer contact, accounting, payroll and so on – quicker and more cost effective. Again, technology can be expensive so may also need to be seen as a long-term investment. New technology will also make additional training necessary so this cost must be taken into account.

New markets

Entry into new markets is often expensive but is seen as an ideal way to sell more products or services. In particular, if these new markets are export markets then there may be considerable costs involved. In addition to travel costs, there will be market research and packaging issues to be resolved. If the new market is, in effect, a new route to market, such as selling via agents or new retail outlets, then there will also be extra costs involved. Again, this can be a long-term investment as new markets rarely produce extra profits in the short term, so finance may be needed to cover these expenses until the new markets start to produce income for the organisation.

New premises

Moving a business from one set of premises to another can be a very expensive and difficult process. Apart from purchasing or renting new premises, extra costs could include removal vans, legal fees, relocation and installation of machinery and equipment (sometimes with specialist help), refurbishment of the new premises, relocation packages for employees (for key employees this could include extra pay, travelling or home removal expenses), advising customers and suppliers about the move and printing new stationery and marketing materials with the new address.

Acquisitions and takeovers

If a business is to take over another business additional finance will usually be required to pay the owners of the business being taken over and also the necessary fees for legal services needed to effect the transfer of assets and so on. Also, amalgamating two businesses can incur extra costs, many of which are similar to those incurred when moving to new premises.

Running costs

Usually day-to-day running costs will be met from current income. However, from time to time this income is not sufficient to meet current expenses and additional finance will be needed to bridge a gap. Finance for running costs may also be required if something out of the ordinary occurs such as machine breakdowns or larger bills than had been allowed for in the cash flow forecast.

Having decided on the need for additional finance to carry out planned developments within an organisation, we can now look at what types of finance may be available.

Types of finance

The type of finance and the origin of this finance will usually be decided by taking a number of factors into account. These include:

- The amount required – the higher the amount, the more limited will be the choices of finance available.
- Current relationship with the organisation's bank – have they already lent to the organisation, do they have confidence in its performance, and do they view it as a good risk?
- Current economic climate – in difficult times, conventional sources of finance may not be available to the organisation.
- The level of risk involved. For risky ventures the sources of finance may be limited as fewer financial institutions will want to take on the risk involved. Consequently, the interest rates charged on ventures like this will be higher.
- The length of time that the finance will be required.

Any one or more of the above factors can dictate – or at least influence – the source of the additional finance. For example, if a small amount of cash is required for a small business then the business owner or their relatives might be the best way to cover the requirement, whereas if a large amount is required for a speculative venture involving a relatively high degree of risk, then a more formal financial institution will more likely be the right source to approach. However, if the organisation's relationship with their usual bank is not very strong then it may be necessary to conduct an extensive search for finance at the right rate.

Different types of finance suit different purposes. The broad categories of types of finance are outlined below.

Current operations

It may be possible to fund smaller projects from the income the organisation generates in the course of business. However, many projects aimed at developing the business will require a greater amount of funding and the categories that follow will then have to be considered.

Loans

Borrowing money (and paying it back with interest) is the main way that most organisations will fund their development activities. There is a variety of sources of such funding, each with their own advantages and disadvantages. These sources include:

Overdraft

This is often available from your bankers. To offer an overdraft facility a bank will need to be confident that the organisation has the wherewithal to repay the outstanding amount. This will include not only a profitable business that will generate sufficient funds to enable the loan to be paid back in a specified time but also a competent management team that can demonstrate relevant experience. It is usually a short-term method of borrowing and is a relatively expensive option. This source of funding should therefore usually be used to cover short-term shortfalls to avoid cash flow problems rather than to fund major projects. The bank or other financial institution offering the overdraft facility will usually set an upper limit and the borrower may trade using the overdraft funds so that the level of borrowing will vary from day to day but must not exceed the limit. If further funds are required it may be necessary to increase the limit.

Mortgage

If the organisation has considerable assets including commercial property it may be possible to raise funding secured against these assets.

Bank loans

Borrowing money and repaying it with interest is a common way of financing business development. Loans may be available from high street banks, finance companies or building societies and interest rates can vary tremendously so research into what is available is essential. Negotiation on both the rate of interest to be charged and the length of time that the loan is spread over may be possible so careful consideration of the requirements of the business is necessary. It is not necessary to keep with your main banking provider for your loan requirements and it is always good practice to obtain quotes from a number of sources – maybe three or four – so that you can be sure of getting the best deal for your organisation. It is also possible to use the services of a mortgage broker or your financial adviser/accountant.

A bank will require a business plan as detailed above that makes a good case for the bank to lend money to the organisation and, in the case of a small, privately owned business, will usually want to see evidence of the owner(s) having invested some of their own money into the enterprise.

This sort of funding, in contrast to that offered in the form of an overdraft (the amount of which may vary over the life of a business) will be for a fixed amount and will usually be for the purchase of assets such as machinery or vehicles and a schedule for repayment will be arranged. Another vital difference between overdrafts and loans is that overdrafts can be cancelled by the bank at any point whereas loans will usually be for an agreed term and, as long as the repayment terms are met, the loan will continue for the agreed period, which may be linked to the life of the item that the loan is required to pay for – usually three or more years.

INSTANT TIP

Avoid unauthorised lenders – sometimes referred to as 'loan sharks' – as the rates of interest may well be prohibitive. This may seem like a quick and easy solution but is not a wise one.

Family and friends

If a business owner is lucky enough to have friends or relatives who have spare cash then it might be possible to borrow from them. The important thing to note about this is that it must be spare cash and not something that they may need in the short term. Too many problems would accompany a loan from a family member, for instance, who had a desperate need for life savings lost if a business is not successful.

Equity

This is a common way that larger organisations raise funding. The investor in the case of a limited company may be a venture capitalist or business angel or, in the case of a public limited company, the general public. This method has the advantage of not being a loan that must be repaid, with interest, at a certain date. Rather it is an investment in the organisation and the return on that investment depends upon the success of the business. An investor in a smaller, private company will often have skills and experience that they can bring to the organisation in addition to the investment and will have a real interest in the success of the project for which the funds are required. As always, there are disadvantages to accompany the advantages. This sort of investment funding is often time consuming and difficult to obtain and will often result in a business owner having to relinquish some control of the organisation.

Also included in this category of funding could be extra cash that a business owner chooses to put into the business to facilitate special projects to expand the business. This money could simply be savings that the business owner has available or loans guaranteed against a house or other personal assets. The risk of losing such an investment should be given very careful consideration.

Leasing

If the development of an organisation is dependent upon acquiring specialised or expensive machinery and equipment, then it is often possible to lease these items through a finance company rather than purchasing them outright. Although this will usually prove a more expensive option than purchasing the required assets, such agreements often include regular maintenance costs and also repairs as necessary. The disadvantage of this method of financing equipment is, of course, that the finance company retains ownership of the item and it will never become an asset of the business.

Grants

Many organisations offer grants for specific purposes to businesses. These include charitable trusts, government agencies and local government. There are two aspects of these grants – discovering what is available and fulfilling the eligibility criteria.

Many grants are given to specific types of business such as manufacturing or to categories of person such as those in rural occupations, unemployed people or people in a particular age range. They may also be given to encourage entrepreneurs in a local area where, for example, extra jobs need to be created. Sometimes funding of this sort has to be 'match-funded', i.e. the organisation will have to invest an equal amount of money into the business or project to be eligible. Although this type of funding has the advantage of being, in effect, a gift rather than having to be paid back in the future, there are often disadvantages in that appropriate grants can be difficult to find (ask government agencies, search online or enquire via local organisations such as Chambers of Commerce), it can take a long time to complete the applications and then for a decision to be made.

All publicly funded finance initiatives for business have recently been drawn together into one scheme – Solutions for Business. This includes finance, grants, loan guarantees, mentoring and information and covers all sorts of business from finance and help for start-ups to advice on exporting or research and development for more established organisations. Visit www.bis.gov.uk or contact your local Business Link for more details. Note that this business advice and funding only applies to England. Different arrangements apply in Scotland, Wales and Northern Ireland.

Research finance

Some types of research and development projects may be of interest to relevant university departments and they may be prepared to fund the research to get involved in ground-breaking projects.

Any of the above sources of finance for a business can be used in isolation but, in reality, most businesses will have a blend of funding sources that they will draw on or implement at different times for different purposes. This will give the business managers the advantage of flexibility and will also reduce the reliance on any one lender and in this way afford the business managers some control over their finances.

Finally, when considering how to raise funding for projects, any organisation should consider their customers and suppliers. Although this may not, at first, seem an obvious choice, it may be possible to make more cash available to the business by getting your customers to pay in advance or getting suppliers to accept longer payment terms. Both of these options will result in cash flow advantages for the business rather than huge sums of money to spend on projects but will be cost effective and not involve risk to the organisation.

Having decided how much and for what purpose the funding is required and what type of finance would be appropriate, the next step will be to consider who to approach. Within each type of finance there will be choices to be made. There are numerous sources of loans, for example, and it is essential to review each one thoroughly. Look for:

- Cost – interest rates and arrangement fees can vary tremendously so shop around for the best deal. A finance institution will quote rates according to its perception of risk so the prospective borrower must present a solid case for any borrowing request to ensure that they secure a good deal.
- Availability – this will vary according to the current economic climate and also to conditions within the lending institution itself so this may be another reason to shop around.
- Reliability and reputation – it is necessary to make sure that you are borrowing from a reputable organisation. Rates from unregistered lenders will usually be higher and the lending term may be unfavourable. You can check that a lender is registered by visiting the Office of Fair Trading's website at www.oft.gov.uk.

When shopping around for finance for a business it can increase chances of success to know what a lender will be looking for. Obviously, any lender will want to know that any loan will be repaid promptly and on time. They will need sufficient detail about the business to be able to make a judgement about the risk they will be taking. They will also need to feel that they are getting a good deal with good terms and a good return on their investment. They will need to have sufficient information about the organisation and what the finance is required for to enable them to assess the risks involved. The aspects of a possible investment opportunity that they will need to be convinced about include:

- An opportunity – has a market niche been identified or has the organisation come up with a good idea?
- The owner or senior management – they will be looking for competent, experienced people in whom they can have confidence.
- The business plan – does the organisation have an understanding of its market and their place in it and does the business plan demonstrate that the systems are in place to make the most of the opportunity?

Anyone who is considering lending money to any organisation will need to know the likelihood of their getting the money back and what they will gain from making the loan. This applies whether the potential lender is a large multinational bank considering a million pound deal or a relative wondering whether to lend a few hundred pounds from their savings. Any organisation wishing to borrow, for whatever reason, will need to make the right case to their potential lender.

INSTANT TIP

Having obtained finance, it is useful to keep in touch with lenders. This can be to reassure them that they will be repaid as agreed or to warn them of potential problems.

Using finance specialists

All but the very smallest of businesses will need specialist financial advice either occasionally or on a regular basis. Using specialists to advise, assist and control when endeavouring to secure additional finance for a business is essential. This assistance can be in the form of your usual accountant, internal experts, bank managers, brokers and other specialist advisers and consultants. Getting the best out of such assistance, which will often incur considerable expense, is vital. Let's look at the various sources of financial advice and assistance.

Accountants

Even small concerns will usually use an accountant to ensure that they comply with legal requirements and also to help them to control their financial situation. Large organisations will, of course, employ a full-time accountant – often in a very senior position – but smaller ones will need to find a self-employed accountant to help them prepare accounts. An accountant may assist with:

- preparing and submitting an annual tax return to HM Revenue and Customs
- preparing PAYE records

- preparing VAT returns
- advising re financial strategy
- preparing final accounts
- auditing final accounts
- filing final accounts with the Registrar of Companies. This is a legal requirement if the organisation is a limited company.
- book-keeping – this can include, for instance, payroll for employees, preparation of invoices, VAT records, checking and paying suppliers' invoices.

Choosing an accountant is an important step. As a minimum, they should possess the appropriate qualification and professional indemnity insurance and charge fees as agreed. It can also be helpful if they are familiar with your business sector and also offer additional services such as advice with funding or specialist tax advice.

Banks

Having a good relationship with the organisation's bankers can be a real advantage in some situations. They should understand your business and the market in which it operates and can be an ideal source of advice on financial strategy. However, they will only loan money to organisations that they consider to be a reasonable risk so, no matter how long and close the relationship with an organisation, there is no guarantee of funds being made available. Also, they will not always be the source of the best deal for an organisation so when looking for additional finance it is essential to approach a number of alternative sources. It is not necessary to limit finance to just one bank.

Consultants and financial advisers

Anyone having difficulty finding the right loan or who needs help putting a case together may find it useful to contact a financial broker. Visit the National Association of Finance Brokers' website at www.nacfb.org for more details.

There are a number of specialist advisers who can assist with loans and finance for people in particular categories such as young or older people, social enterprises or members of certain communities. A search on the internet will find many details of such organisations, some of which are mentioned in the Further Information section at the back of this book.

NB As Sharia law does not permit the charging or paying of interest, loans for Muslim business owners are available via specialist advisers. For more details visit www.islamic-bank.com.

Business consultants working with organisations to improve various aspects of their business, for example productivity or customer service, may well be involved in financial aspects of the business and may advise about raising additional finance for projects that they discover are necessary to improve the business operations.

SUMMARY

This chapter tackled the very important subject of finance. First, we looked at how to prepare a budget as a plan of how to meet the targets that have been set for the business. A budget should quantify goals for income and expenditure and ensure that finances are under control. It should also be closely allied to the business plan.

We saw that a budget should include both direct and indirect costs and sales forecasts. Monitoring budgets against actual income and expenditure and performance

(Continued)

(Continued)

year on year will enable management to arrive at effective decisions and for corrective action to be taken.

Next we looked at the importance of managing cash flow and expenditure to keep plans on target and at when and how the responsibility for budgets may be delegated.

Obtaining finance was dealt with next, including identifying the need, types of finance and possible sources. Additional finance may be required to enter new markets, produce new products, to take over another business, to facilitate a move to new premises or to invest in new machinery or technology for use in the business as well as for day-to-day running of the business. The main types of additional finance include loans, equity, leasing and grants.

Finally in this section we considered when to use financial specialists and how to choose one.

ACTION CHECKLIST

1. Consider the last budget produced for your department or area of work – did it closely follow the business plan?
2. Have costs and sales both increased year on year in your organisation?
3. What corrective action was necessary following the last review of the budget for your department?
4. What sources of finance has your organisation used in the last five years?
5. What was the additional finance used for and did it produce the desired results?

03

How is technology best used and promoted?

Using information technology (IT) can improve the way business is done. While some organisations use technology to a very high level of sophistication, others use only the most basic applications. The most important aspect in either case is to use IT to ensure that the organisation works as effectively as possible given the work to be done and the budget available. Businesses making the best use of IT will use it to develop new systems and also to take advantage of new opportunities to gain a competitive edge. A fairly recent example of this is the trend towards online sales. Just a few years ago selling online – e-commerce – was innovative, expensive and risky but the businesses that invested in the technology to facilitate selling online are now reaping the benefits and the ones that held back are now having to race to catch up. So, it can be seen that the use of IT must form a central part of how an organisation uses its resources and this chapter will now look at how this can be achieved

What do we mean by technology?

In answer to that question, most people would say 'computers' and, of course, that is a very basic, but correct, answer. Although IT is run by computers, its uses in business are many and varied. These include:

- Preparation of documents – letters, reports, invoices, etc. One of the many benefits of word processing is that documents can be made to look professional quite easily.
- Electronic communication – emails are an invaluable part of most organisations' communications both internally and externally. It is also possible to use the internet to make cheaper overseas telephone calls and the technology facilitates the use of webcams so that two people can see one another while talking on the phone.
- Record keeping – useful in every department.
- Database management – details of customers, suppliers, employees, products and so on can be recorded and then intricate reports produced that would have taken much longer – if they were possible at all – with a manual system.
- Accountancy systems – software packages to carry out accounting processes including everything from receiving an order to preparing final accounts.
- Payroll preparation – accurate preparation of payslips, PAYE and analysis.
- Order processing – orders can either be keyed in by staff or facilities may be given to large customers to enter their orders direct onto internal systems; then the order can be fulfilled and tracked. Both supplier and customer can have access to the order system.

- Information management – information can be disseminated and systems allowing restricted access can be installed.
- Production machinery setting and operation – many machine operations are controlled by computers.
- Business process redesign – process re-engineering relies heavily on technology such as shared databases to deliver results and can ensure a better work flow using computerised systems and information.
- Enterprise resource planning – making the best use of the organisation's resources will ensure improved performance. For example, stock control and purchasing systems can be shared with suppliers thereby reducing stock and ensuring resources are available as and when required.
- Company websites – all but the smallest of enterprises has a website. These can serve a variety of purposes from simply giving contact details and brief details about an organisation to being the main contact with their customers.
- Online sales and bookings – online sales are growing and are a vital part of many organisations' income.
- Online research – searching the internet for all sorts of information.
- Online marketing – a web presence has become an essential part of many organisation's marketing strategy.
- Use of social networking sites – promoting business, building a brand and sharing information with other members of such sites, e.g. LinkedIn.
- Sharing information via internal or external networks.
- Supply chain management – this encompasses many of the processes that would previously have been carried out via paper-based systems such as stock checking, triggering and tracking orders.

● Mobile working – mobile phones, remote internet access and systems allowing communications and remote access to information and internal systems via the internet has made it easier for employees to work away from a central location.
● Satellite navigation – this has made many delivery drivers' jobs much easier and also facilitates better planning.

Although this list is long, it is not exhaustive. New uses and new software are continually being introduced and it is a continual necessity to keep abreast of new developments. However, the most important aspect of the use of IT in business is whether or not it is appropriate for the organisation. It is essential that the organisation's need for technologies is assessed at the outset and then its use monitored on a regular basis to ensure the most effective use is made of available technology.

Assessing what technology is needed

The first action to take in introducing or updating IT in an organisation is to assess the needs of the business. There is little point in a small business with only a few customers installing an expensive, all-singing, all-dancing invoicing system if all they have to do is prepare five or six invoices per month. Similarly, an organisation with thousands of customers buying small amounts several times per month would be hard-pressed to function without a sophisticated invoicing system and the associated control of stock and credit.

A thorough examination of the way business is carried out is vital before any new systems are introduced or changes made to existing computerised systems. Look at:

- the systems currently in use
- what is going well
- what needs improvement
- who will use the systems
- what training will be needed
- the money available for IT improvements
- what cost savings may be possible
- possible impacts on customers
- timescales.

With this information it should be possible to decide where new IT would benefit the organisation, how much is available to finance it and what would be the possible problems that would impact on various areas of the business. The gains from introducing new IT into a business can be enormous but these must be balanced against the cost of the proposed system and the work that will have to be put in within the organisation to ensure that the new system works correctly. Gains to be made from the introduction of new IT include:

- increased productivity
- better communications – internally and externally – communications can be made quicker and cheaper
- more cost effective marketing solutions
- increased sales
- decreased costs, e.g. it's cheaper to send an email than a letter
- quicker and more comprehensive accounting data
- making better use of existing systems, e.g. by networking them.

Usually IT solutions are introduced to solve a problem identified within a business but care should be taken not to view the problem in isolation. The introduction of new systems using IT almost invariably has an impact on other areas. More or fewer staff may be necessary to run the new system efficiently, or one department's work using a new system may cause problems for others. For example, if an accounts department starts to use a new system to produce reports based on the invoices they have produced, other departments may receive those reports in a different format, which may cause them to have to change their way of working. Also, customers may be adversely affected, and even if this effect is only in the installation and settling down periods, action must be taken to limit the effect and to advise them of the reasons for it.

So, taking care that the introduction of technology does not have negative effects, the various departments involved can gather information about the possible solutions to the problem identified. This group could include, where appropriate, the heads of the departments specifically affected in addition to, perhaps, the purchasing manager, the accountant and the IT manager as appropriate.

INSTANT TIP

It is vital that any purchases of IT equipment and software are compatible with existing systems. Many hours can be lost trying to make systems work together and it may be best to take an expert's advice before deciding on a specific system.

Having assessed and decided what technology is appropriate for the organisation, the next decision will be how to acquire it. Most hardware can be either bought or leased and the decision will depend on many things including the cost of the proposed improvements, finance available and the expected life span of the equipment.

Monitoring your use of technology

There are a number of aspects of technology use that must be monitored and systems should be put in place to ensure that regular checks are made. Consider the following:

- Is it up to date? It does not necessarily have to be the most up-to-date technology available but it should suit the purpose at the time and a regular check will ensure that this is still the case. Continuing to use systems when there is a better, more efficient system available can be a false economy.
- Is it still fulfilling the purpose for which it was introduced? Being aware of the objectives of the introduction of any technology being used in an organisation will ensure that you can assess its effectiveness. Have the benefits that were envisaged been realised? And if not, why not?
- Security – check that the IT security policy is still workable and is being actively used. Threats from within the organisation and from outside it should be covered, e.g. protection against viruses coming into the organisation's IT systems or from data theft by employees and others who have access to it.
- The organisation must comply with the Data Protection Act 1998 so policies should be in place to avoid offences in this area.
- Have there been developments in the technology available that would benefit the organisation? It may be that changes have occurred which would mean that some tasks could be undertaken in a more efficient way and it is a manager's job to be aware of such changes and then to decide how to use them within his department.

- Have there been changes within the organisation that would mean that different technology would be of use? For example, if the customer base has increased significantly, dealing with customers may be made easier and more cost effective by using relationship management software.
- Is the maintenance system that is in place sufficient to keep things running smoothly? If significant changes in the numbers of people using the technology are planned, it might be useful to outsource this function. Reports of down time of any part of the system should be monitored to spot trends so that problems can be dealt with before too much time is lost.
- Is the information on all systems kept up to date? It is often found that employees will work around problems in a system – including incorrect details held on file – changing the way they work or spending time substituting the correct information and thereby wasting time that could be better spent on other tasks.
- Don't forget to check technology used by people who are not office-based. This might include delivery drivers, sales people, engineers and so on.
- Are employees using any technology adequately trained? In addition to asking managers this question it is always informative to ask the employees themselves.
- Are employees able to work safely when using technology? Check their work stations, seating, lighting and so on to ensure that the risk of injury or discomfort is minimised.
- Do employees fully understand the organisation's policy regarding use of the internet while at work? Employers need to ensure that their internet connection is not used to gain unauthorised access to sites that are not work related or for illegal purposes.

As always, monitoring is not enough. After any assessment of this kind it is necessary to consider what has been discovered and then take any corrective action that may be necessary.

INSTANT TIP

Security is a vital part of IT in business. Systems should be in place to monitor security to prevent loss to the organisation.

Improving your use of technology

Many organisations will set up their systems when they set up a small company and then not make any major changes to their use of IT despite the business itself going through enormous changes in its lifetime and despite the considerable improvements made to the IT on offer. They will muddle along, perhaps occasionally investing in new software or a few PCs or printers, patching up a system that is no longer fit for purpose. This sort of 'fire fighting' is, to a certain extent, understandable as most senior managers have plenty to do and may have an attitude of 'if it isn't broken, don't fix it'. However, this could well be a false economy in terms of both time and money. Efficient use of technology can pay dividends in terms of the results produced and how long it takes to produce them.

An example of this would be the internet connection that an organisation uses. Without the available upgrades to a service that can provide high speed, reliable connection, an organisation can waste a lot of time waiting for large files, websites and so on to load. They will also not be able to take advantage of the additional areas that such a service may open up to them. With a high speed connection many applications that will help to manage the business and its suppliers in 'real time', online, can be utilised. This can be as simple as being in constant contact with customers, suppliers and employees via email and shared information, or it can be a more complicated change involving expensive software to provide information and forecasts using data as it is entered on to the systems. Software systems are available that will enable the following:

Analysis of information

This can include sales orders, stock levels and markets. An efficient IT system can produce vast amounts of data and from this produce reports that will assist in the management of a business.

Planning stock levels

Stock levels can be adjusted according to the stock that goes out and then the IT system can automatically generate orders to suppliers or issue requests for deliveries.

Enterprise Resource Planning

Sophisticated IT systems that will plan activities throughout the organisation are available. Enterprise Resource Planning systems can link all areas of the systems used within an organisation – purchase orders, sales, stock levels, dispatches and invoicing – and then plan the necessary actions depending on the details received. Installing a system of this type is a major change for any organisation and uses expensive IT software and engages the services of specialist consultants. It will take many months to install and will require extensive staff training but it will force an examination of all the processes undertaken within a business that would not otherwise have been undertaken and should result in major efficiency savings.

In order to decide how technology can best be used it is necessary to consider the use of technology as a whole within the business. A strategy for IT use that covers the entire organisation, its aims and objectives and its vision, will mean that the entire business gets the very best out of the investment of time and money that will be made in the technology. This strategy should plan the use of technology to cover a period of years and will consider the following:

- Where is the organisation going? What are the aims, its vision, plans to enter different markets and so on?
- What will it need, in terms of investment in technology, to achieve its objectives?
- If expansion is planned, is the current IT set-up capable of being expanded? If not, then an alternative should be mapped out.
- Will the organisation employ more or fewer people in the future?
- If remote working is used within the organisation, consider the type of network that is needed.
- Could there be requirements in the future for remote working?
- Does the expertise to manage the technology requirements exist within the organisation or will it be necessary to engage a specialist?
- The budget available for any planned upgrades or expansion and the maintenance of existing systems.
- Will any necessary hardware be purchased or leased?
- Will the software needed be a standard product (usually the case for small companies and many larger ones) or one that is designed especially for the organisation (an expensive option usually limited to major organisations)?

- What are the future training requirements in respect of the use of IT?
- How will the system be maintained?
- What systems, hardware and software are currently in use? Are they nearing the end of their useful life? This can happen when a software developer withdraws technical support for some of its software applications.

This sort of strategy requires careful planning and is usually carried out alongside writing the business plan. It is difficult to write an IT strategy without a business plan as the two should mirror the same aims and objectives and writing a business plan without considering its implications for the future use of technology would be unwise.

Assessing the organisation's IT needs alongside the business plan will produce the following benefits:

- There will be uniformity in the systems used throughout the organisation.
- It prevents 'knee jerk' reactions when problems come along. It is always tempting to purchase a solution to a problem but if there is an IT policy in place all purchases must comply with it.
- Data can be shared throughout the organisation.
- Staff can all be trained to use the same systems.
- Systems support is easier with a uniform policy.

Having done the research, a comprehensive IT strategy can be drawn up. This should include details of present and future requirements along with plans for the implementation of new systems and the maintenance of existing ones. This will cover the possible use of specialists or new staff and also the training needs of current employees. At this point cost estimates should be obtained to ensure that the planned policy is feasible given the budget available.

Following a comprehensive review of IT requirements and the drawing up of an IT strategy, many aspects of IT use can be improved. This will encompass simple changes to existing ways of working and go right through to the most complicated of changes involving the implementation of entire systems. These improvements may include:

- Using email – encouraging employees to use email as a routine way of dealing with their colleagues rather than memos, and also with customers and suppliers, is a simple measure but will produce savings in time and also reduce the use of paper within the business. But don't forget that occasionally either a face-to-face conversation or a phone call can be the best way to deal with a particular issue.
- Developing a series of templates for word processing documents that will save time and also give a more professional and uniform look to materials sent out by the whole organisation.
- Developing a website that can serve many purposes – making information available to people inside and outside the organisation, facilitating sales enquiries and so on.
- Online sales – this is an increasing market for many large companies and is also an effective way for many smaller organisations to enter the market without having to expand their sales force.
- Facilitating remote working.
- Stock control systems.
- Payroll systems.
- Accounting software that can produce invoices, reminders, statements and so on automatically.
- The use of manufacturing machinery that is set up at the point of installation then will automatically replicate the process via computerised controls.

- Linking the organisation's systems with suppliers or customers to automate ordering processes, payments and so on.
- Video conferencing – this can eliminate the need to hire expensive meeting venues and enables staff to attend meetings without wasting time and money travelling to a central point.

It can be seen therefore that improvements in efficiency and effectiveness can be achieved with a more organised and planned use of IT within an organisation. Some changes my require help from outside the organisation so the next section deals with selecting and working with specialists in this area.

INSTANT TIP

Always be sure that the Data Protection Act is complied with. Developing a written policy that everyone is aware of is essential.

Working with technology specialists

Although it is possible for an organisation to deal with all its own arrangements and use of information technology – purchasing computers, printers and software, building a website, running complicated systems, controlling data, supporting staff who work away from the main office, setting up networks and ensuring compliance with legislation – many companies of all sizes decide that they are not technology experts and choose to get help from specialists outside the organisation. Specialists can provide help not only to manage the day-to-day aspects of using technology within a business but also to solve problems that may occur from time to time. The systems that specialists will be able to advise on can offer improvements in performance. The problems that they may be able to resolve include:

● Lost data – computer crashes can result in a disastrous loss of data. However, this can be avoided with a system of regular back-ups and knowing how to retrieve data.
● Inefficient filing – many computer users do not have a system of naming and storing files and many hours can be lost in looking for vital pieces of information.
● Computer security – experts can quickly provide solutions to the prevention of viruses and keeping company data safe from hackers.
● Computer downtime – the problems caused by a computer crash can be huge and prolonged. Being unable to produce invoices or dispatch orders efficiently can be disastrous both for immediate cash flow and also for the organisation's reputation.
● Regular maintenance – keeping computers working well can prevent major losses and downtime.

All of these hassles can be avoided by working with people who know how to use technology effectively – IT specialists. Although resolving problems such as these will undoubtedly result in greater efficiency and free up time for employees dealing with problems caused by inefficient use of technology, IT experts will also be able to offer many proactive solutions where technology can be used to take organisations to a different level in terms of how they do business. For example, many businesses would benefit from using customer relationship management systems or their operations could be improved by all their computers, printers and so on being networked. Let's look at the sorts of solutions for improving a business that can be offered by IT specialists.

Customer relationship management

IT specialists can advise on the choice and use of software that will allow a company to organise and automate its contacts with customers. This will ensure that not only are customers contacted frequently and in a professional manner but also that everyone in the organisation will do this in the same way. Such a system can also produce reports about customer contact, responses and orders, resulting in a greater knowledge of what customers want. This, in turn, can result in increased business via an improved approach to sales and marketing. Without this sort of software system, many organisations' contact with customers is haphazard. This can result in lost sales and in the organisation's reputation suffering. Efficient use of such a system will result in several advantages for the organisation including improved retention of customers, increased orders and a more uniform approach to sales and marketing plus greater information becoming available that will enable managers to spot trends and adjust the product offer accordingly.

Networking

The linking of computers and devices such as printers within an organisation is often referred to as a network. Getting help in setting up a network is a very common reason for calling in specialists. Linking in this way produces a number of advantages:

- sharing hardware (printers, etc.) among many users
- sharing data – everyone can have access (subject to security and confidentiality provisions which may be built into the system) to the same documents and data
- improved communications between employees
- better information being available and easier access to it

- better use of resources – a printer can be used by all employees linked into a network, so that each individual does not need a dedicated printer.

Remote working

Many workers have worked away from a central office for many years. In particular many sales people for large organisations have traditionally been based at home and have only gone into the main office for scheduled meetings rather than on a daily basis. With the improvement in available technologies this trend has increased and now encompasses many workers who would usually have been office-based. Computers, email, the internet and mobile telephony have all played an important part in this so that, for instance, a worker can be home based but still be able to do work online and communicate in a variety of ways with the central office.

The advantages that these sorts of IT help can bring to an organisation are many and varied:

- improved customer relations
- increased sales
- better results from marketing efforts
- improved communication within the organisation
- a decrease in costs – and more control over costs
- staff can concentrate on their core tasks rather than fixing computer glitches
- a more professional image for the organisation
- facilitating remote working
- more flexible working patterns
- a decrease in time-consuming routine tasks
- increased productivity.

It is apparent that engaging the services of technology specialists rather than going it alone will bring appreciable benefits to an organisation.

From the above it is obvious that many improvements can be made by increasing the use of technology with the help of IT specialists. However, some of these solutions can be expensive so careful selection of an appropriate specialist is necessary. Finding and choosing a technology specialist can be difficult. The best way, as always, is by personal recommendation from someone in a similar organisation but this is not always possible, so some research will be necessary. The choice of specialist will obviously depend mainly on the task to be undertaken but the following will also play a part in the decision:

- The experience of the specialist – evidence should be sought of experience of dealing with similar problems and installing solutions in other organisations. References should be available and should be checked out. Engaging someone to deal with the organisation's data or to change the way in which it deals with its customers is an important step. In addition to competence in the specialist area, confidentiality is an important aspect of such work. A good relationship is necessary so building up trust by way of obtaining references is essential.
- Reputation of the specialist – ask around, find out if the specialist is easy to work with and achieves the right results. Reliability and, as mentioned previously, confidentiality are important attributes to look for.
- Size of the organisation and the work to be carried out – a small company wanting to network five computers, a laser printer and a fax machine, for example, will probably need a different specialist to that needed by a large multinational company wanting to set up a network involving hundreds of computers and so on.

● Size of the specialist organisation – as above, a large company will be able to tackle larger, more complex issues than a small company who may be right for simple computer security issues, for example.
● The nature of the problem – as in all fields there are specialists within the area of computer solutions. Some will deal exclusively with networked solutions and others may offer day-to-day help or may supply customer relationship management systems.
● The budget – this will often dictate the type of solution and therefore the type of specialist organisation that can be engaged.

As with any other major supplier to an organisation, a comprehensive agreement should be put in place that will set out the terms and conditions of the agreement between the organisation and the specialist. This should include details of the service to be supplied, how long it will be supplied for, who owns any equipment used, what should be done in the event of a disagreement or complaint and how the contract will end. This will avoid misunderstandings and make clear just what the responsibilities of both parties are.

SUMMARY

In this chapter we concentrated on the many uses of technology in organisations from preparing invoices and letters and sending emails to websites and mobile working. We also looked at how its use can be improved.

A thorough examination of how business is carried out is necessary before any new systems are introduced. Used effectively, IT can solve problems, improve productivity and enable better communications. Any new systems and their security must be monitored to ensure they are up to date and continue to fulfil their purpose.

(Continued)

(Continued)

The use of IT can be improved in a number of ways including analysis of information, facilitating remote working and planning activities throughout the organisation. Any changes should be made in conjunction with the business plan so that the changes will assist in achieving the goals detailed in the business plan.

Next we looked at working with technical specialists. They can help to manage a number of IT uses ranging from the day-to-day use and maintenance to installing large IT-based solutions such as networking the computers and devices within an organisation or customer relationship management systems.

ACTION CHECKLIST

1. How many ways do you use IT in your day-to-day work role?
2. Are there ways that the use of IT could be improved in your organisation? If so, how could these changes be introduced?
3. Is the use of IT in your organisation monitored?
4. How do the IT systems used in your organisation further the aims of the business plan?
5. Does your organisation make use of IT specialists? If so, how, and if not, how do you think your use of IT could be improved by specialists?

04

How can you ensure health and safety requirements are met?

High standards in health and safety management are vital not only in ensuring that employees do not come to any harm while at work but also in order to satisfy the legislation that is designed to do just that. The responsibility for these standards belongs, in legal terms, to the management of the organisation but, on a day-to-day basis, everyone within the organisation must play their part.

Health and safety regulations exist to protect two groups of people and organisations. First, employees and members of the public are protected from reckless or careless behaviour by others. Second, they protect the organisation itself in that, if the managers and/or owners of the business comply with the regulations – and therefore with the advice contained therein – they will be less likely to cause injury to others. If these laws are not complied with and the result is injury or loss then any organisation can be fined heavily and legal cases may be brought against the organisation for

damages. Sometimes health and safety may be seen as something that has 'gone too far' but there are very good reasons for the emphasis on it.

If you have any responsibility in your organisation – maybe you are a safety representative, a department manager or even the business owner – then the first thing to do in order to ensure that health and safety requirements are met is to become fully familiar with all the regulations that apply to your organisation. Performance in safety matters is often seen as the responsibility of a specialist officer within the organisation or, alternatively, the organisation uses the services of a specialist consultant in these matters. However, this does not absolve management from responsibility. Attitudes to health and safety matters will filter down from the top of any management structure so management taking it seriously is a first step to ensuring the requirements are met. Even managers who do not have direct operational responsibility will be able to exert influence on the attitude to health and safety that exists within an organisation as they will be involved in:

- developing and displaying a responsible attitude to health and safety, for example, ensuring that health and safety is on the agenda at all general planning meetings, board meetings and so on
- developing a health and safety policy within the organisation
- setting up systems that support a responsible approach to health and safety
- making the appropriate resources available
- developing a clear chain of command and communication so that everyone is aware of their responsibilities in the area of health and safety
- appointing and authorising members of staff to put in place the appropriate health and safety measures

- maintaining a high profile in terms of how they portray health and safety within the organisation. This could take the form of gaining publicity for any new measures in this area, giving health and safety equal importance with other matters such as sales or production and discussing their approach with members of staff whenever the opportunity arises.

The basic principle behind all health and safety regulations and measures that are recommended is that of protection. All health and safety measures must be aimed at preventing injury and loss. A bit of forethought and planning plus simple, straightforward systems put in place will be to the advantage of everyone who comes into contact with an organisation.

INSTANT TIP

If you employ anyone you will usually have to have employers' liability compulsory insurance. A free leaflet is available on the subject from www.hsebooks.co.uk.

What is your organisation's approach to health and safety?

Health and safety must be managed. A rigorous approach on the part of senior managers to health and safety will determine the attitudes held throughout the organisation. This approach can be seen in the following behaviour:

- Senior managers showing personal commitment to health and safety matters.

- Setting high standards for health and safety performance.
- Providing the necessary resources to comply with health and safety policies.
- Making all department managers responsible for safety performance in their own areas.
- Raising the profile of these matters – in formal meetings and when visiting departments at all levels.

It is important for all organisations to ensure that these matters are not just a matter of theory – i.e. paid lip service – but that achieving high safety standards is one of the stated aims of the business. However, any health and safety strategy should not be there simply for the sake of complying with regulations and legislation, nor should it be something that drives the business and gets in the way of profit or improvement. Instead it should be designed to ensure that a business is run efficiently without endangering staff, the public or anyone else who comes into contact with the organisation. There is also a very important benefit to any organisation in that it can be a powerful tool for staff welfare and motivation.

So, does your organisation have an effective health and safety policy in place? This can be kept quite simple. It needs to set out who does what in relation to health and safety and then to explain how they should do it and when. There is a sample form that can be downloaded from the Health & Safety Executive (HSE) website (www.hse.co.uk) which, when completed, forms a health and safety policy for any organisation.

Employers have a duty to involve employees (or employees' health and safety representatives) in health and safety matters and there is no doubt that a high level of involvement on the part of employees will result in a more effective approach to health and safety in any organisation.

INSTANT TIP

All organisations that employ five or more people must have a written health and safety policy.

Meeting statutory requirements

Health and safety laws and regulations are there to ensure that the public is not put in danger by anything that businesses do and to ensure that employers provide a satisfactory working environment for their employees.

Obligations are put upon all employers by a number of Acts of Parliament and regulations:

- The Health and Safety at Work Act 1974.
- The Workplace (Health, Safety and Welfare) Regulations 1992.
- The Management of Health and Safety at Work Regulations 1999.
- Health and Safety (Consultation with Employees) Regulations 1996.
- Safety Representatives and Safety Committees Regulations 1977.

While employees (such as a health and safety manager or departmental manager) can be given responsibility for doing the work to comply with these regulations, the ultimate responsibility for compliance – and for the effects of non-compliance – remains with the employer.

Organisations will have to carry out a variety of tasks in complying with the relevant regulations. These include:

- creating a written safety policy (where there is in excess of five employees). **NB** Even where there are fewer than five employees, this can still be done and is usually a useful step
- developing management systems that incorporate health and safety requirements
- providing equipment that is safe
- providing adequate supervision
- carrying out risk assessments
- providing health and safety training
- providing personal protective equipment (where appropriate) for which no charge should be made to employees
- having access to a qualified health and safety adviser – as stated previously, this could be a specialist who is not an employee or a member of staff whose duties include the implementation and monitoring of health and safety systems
- maintaining equipment and premises to a safe standard
- recognising union safety representatives (where a workplace has a union presence)
- implementing a monitoring system to ensure standards are being met
- making all safety arrangements known to all employees.

The aim of complying with the regulations is so that safety measures are taken before an accident happens. Obviously, if an accident does occur then investigations must be carried out and, in certain instances, reported to the HSE.

INSTANT TIP

Although the *responsibility* for health and safety of employees cannot be delegated, the *work* involved in carrying out the tasks involved can be delegated to employees.

Although the main burden of care is with the employer, the regulations do not ignore the duties of employees, the general public and others such as suppliers, landlords, neighbours and visitors involved with the organisation in some way. Reasonable standards of behaviour and care so that accidents do not occur and that they comply with safety measures put in place by employers are expected. Specifically, the duties of employees are:

- To cooperate with their employers in order to comply with statutory requirements.
- To take reasonable care of themselves and others who may be affected by their actions.
- Not to interfere with safety equipment, etc., that has been provided by their employers to comply with health and safety legislation.
- To report any incidents or problems that may affect health and safety performance.

The laws and regulations relating to health and safety are enforced (and inspections are carried out) by the HSE and by local authorities according to the type of premises. Broadly, the HSE deals with factories, building sites and farms, while local authorities will inspect and advise shops, pubs, restaurants, hotels, offices and leisure facilities. Inspectors from the HSE or the local authority will visit workplaces to ensure that regulations are being followed and will advise employers how to comply and how to improve their safety performance.

INSTANT TIP

A poster must be displayed in any premises where people are employed. Alternatively staff can be supplied with their own copy of a booklet entitled *Health & Safety Law: what you should know*, which is available from HSE Books (Tel. 0845 345 0055).

Developing a written health and safety policy

As we said previously all organisations employing more than five employees have a duty to have a written health and safety policy and it is also useful to smaller organisations to write down their intention to implement such a policy and also the arrangements that have been made for doing so. A safety policy should include:

- a statement of the aims of the organisation in relation to health and safety
- details of the arrangements that exist for fulfilling the aims of the organisation's health and safety policy – this will include all procedures and provisions relating to health and safety
- details of the measures that are in place for consulting employees regarding health and safety matters
- information about where employees can obtain competent safety advice
- the name of the director who is responsible for complying with health and safety legislation
- details of the responsibilities of all the directors and employees who are in charge of implementing and enforcing the policy.

This written policy should be signed and dated by the person in charge of the organisation and be brought to the attention of all employees. It will need to be reviewed on a regular basis and re-issued when amendments are made.

Identifying and evaluating hazards and risks

Risk assessment is an essential part (and legal requirement) of any health and safety policy. This involves identifying possible hazards that give rise to any risk to employees, suppliers, visitors, delivery drivers and so on, then assessing these hazards to take action to eliminate them if possible or at least to reduce or control them.

INSTANT TIP

If there are more than five employees there is also a duty to record the risk assessments – not just to carry them out.

Risk assessments should be carried out by an assessor who is familiar with the work processes and with the premises in which the risks exist. An assessor should also, of course, be conversant with the relevant health and safety legislation and have some experience of the standards that apply generally in the particular industry or type of workplace.

The identification of possible hazards before an accident has happened is central to any meaningful safety policy. There are many ways of doing this including:

Safety audits

These are detailed, pre-arranged checks of a work area carried out to identify and record all types of hazard. Comprehensive reports are usually made out and often a system of scoring is used to give a basis for improvement.

Safety inspections

Inspections are usually less detailed than audits and will consider a work area in terms of the general approach to accident prevention. They are limited to a specific work area and all defects found in such inspections must be followed up with action. This action must be seen to be taken and should be checked up on at the next safety inspection in that area.

Safety inspections can also take the form of tours around a larger work area or a route through a factory or other premises. These need to be carefully planned to ensure full coverage of all premises and, again, careful follow-up is necessary.

Alternatively, rather than being centred on a work area, safety inspections or tours can concentrate on a particular type of hazard. So, for example, a system of regular checks of stairways and walkways, fire safety or use of chemicals throughout the organisation can be instigated. This needs careful planning to ensure that all types of hazard are covered on a regular basis but, carried out properly, it can be useful in allowing detailed examination of specific hazards.

Fire risk assessments

Avoiding the risk of fires in business premises is an important part of any health and safety policy. Not only may lives be lost and injuries sustained as a result of such fires but they also have high costs in terms of damage and lost working time so being aware of, and minimising, fire risk is essential for any business.

Environment checks

Where chemicals used in a work area may be present in the atmosphere, a system of checks will usually be in place to monitor concentrations. This may entail the use of expensive instruments and results will be monitored with an alarm raised if concentrations go above a specified, safe level. **NB** Some organisations that use dangerous chemicals may be required to hold a licence or to be registered with their local authority.

Accident reports

An important part of any safety policy is the recording of all accidents, however minor. These reports can then be discussed at a health and safety meeting in order to decide on preventative measures.

Many organisations, especially those dealing with hazardous chemicals or processes, keep a score of the number of days since an accident and display this total prominently. This can act as a target for employees in the relevant work areas.

It is also good policy to keep records of 'near misses' as these, although they do not cause injury or loss, will be a good pointer as to where action needs to be taken to improve safety performance.

Day-to-day management

It is important that safety plays a large part in day-to-day management of the organisation. With regular and disciplined follow-up of all safety inspections and accident reports, a culture that places health and safety at high priority is developed. It should be possible to ensure that health and safety is not viewed as just the concern of senior management or of a specialist adviser but is part of the job of everyone employed in the organisation. There is more about how health and safety must play a part in day-to-day management in the section on implementing health and safety measures below.

Employee involvement

Employees can be encouraged to be involved in safety matters in a number of ways. Safety committees that have a designated number of staff members can be formed, with regular meetings being held to discuss accidents and safety measures, or they can report safety incidents to line management on a day-to-day basis. In either case, management must behave in a way that will ensure full participation. This means ensuring that there is no fear of reprisals or blame for reporting a safety incident and that action is seen to be taken when matters of concern are reported.

All of these measures to assess risks are simple to put into practice and a combination of some or all of these methods will ensure that risks are detected.

The hazards and risks that all these measures should be in place to detect, report and remedy are many and varied. They include:

- Slips and trips – this is the most common cause of accidents at work and can result from uneven floors or items such as packaging materials being left around. This type of risk is especially prevalent in restaurants and shops where not only do things get spilled on floors but also members of the public are vulnerable.
- Exposure to hazardous substances – this can be something as simple as cleaning materials. Suppliers of hazardous substances must provide safety information to users.

- Manual handling – injuries caused by lifting even relatively light objects are something to look out for.
- Asbestos (the most common cause of work-related fatal disease) is often found when maintenance and repair work is being carried out. If asbestos is found in any building or workplace it is necessary to call in specialist operators to remove it as disturbing it may release extremely harmful fibres into the atmosphere.
- Use of display screens – repeated or long use of computer screens can cause strain leading to back injuries, eye strain and repetitive strain injuries (RSI). These can be avoided by making sure that work stations are correctly laid out and that staff take regular breaks.
- Stress – the HSE defines this as 'the adverse reaction people have to excessive pressure or other types of demand placed on them' and can be the cause of low morale in the workplace, decreased productivity, absenteeism and poor staff retention.
- High levels of noise – this can cause hearing loss so ear protectors may be necessary.
- Falls from a height – often from ladders and as a result of using the incorrect equipment or using it incorrectly.
- Fire risk – this is obviously increased when working with flammable products but every organisation is at risk of loss from fire on its premises. The local fire authority will give advice on fire alarms, prevention measures, extinguishers and so on.
- Use of machinery and equipment – this includes any items that an employer may supply to an employee such as ladders, hand tools, lifting equipment and all types of machinery. Guidelines for their use will be necessary.
- Transport at work – this will include vans, cars, fork lift trucks, dump trucks, HGVs and all sorts of plant vehicles and could endanger not only the vehicle's user but also other employees and passers-by.

- Vibration damage – often to hands and arms but can also affect backs, legs and heads.
- Use of electricity – most accidents relating to electricity occur as a result of contact with overhead or underground cables but equipment that is used every day can also present danger. Small electrical items and all machinery should be checked regularly.
- Radiation – risks here can range from sun damage on skin to damage from X-ray machinery.
- Maintenance and building work – an employer is responsible not only for the safety of his employees but also for contactors and others who may be called in to do building and maintenance work.

As you can see, the list of risks that may be present in the workplace is almost limitless and, although risk assessment is vital, it is just one step in the process of ensuring that effective health and safety measures are in place. The next, equally vital, step is to implement the necessary measures.

Implementing health and safety measures

Risk assessment is the first step towards the implementation of effective safety measures in any business. When risks have been correctly identified systems can then be put in place to ensure the risk of accidents is minimised. The final step is to monitor these systems.

As we saw from the list above, risks can be found in and around almost anything in the workplace. When assessing risk you are looking for anything that could cause an injury and this could range from something left in the wrong place that someone could trip over to badly maintained vehicles or equipment. Risk assessments will have to be carried out both during and outside working hours. When examining work areas when they are not being used there will be a chance to take the time to spot all sorts of hazards that may lead to harm. However, it is also essential that the work area is examined when work is in progress as it is only then that it is possible to see how people are working. So, for example, you might spot trip hazards when the work area is clear and unused but it will only be possible to see potential causes of injury from lifting when someone is actually doing the lifting.

Having identified risks in the workplace it is then necessary to put in place systems that will ensure these risks are managed and, as far as possible, eradicated. These systems will include some or all of the following:

- Planned maintenance.
- Safe systems of work developed in consultation with workers and with health and safety representatives or experts to provide a formal framework that takes into account hazards and risks that have been identified.
- The provision where necessary of personal protective equipment such as ear protectors, hi-visibility vests, boots with reinforced toe caps, etc.

- Elimination whenever possible of any hazardous operation, work practice or materials.
- Examination of the use of safer materials, machinery and processes.
- Training.
- Emergency procedures/drills.
- First aid procedures and equipment.

An important part of this health and safety management will be communication with employees. This can be done by:

- regular health and safety meetings
- posters in the workplace
- newsletters
- the example shown by the management team – good maintenance procedures and a positive, proactive attitude to health and safety must be apparent to employees
- practise of emergency drills.

Following the identification, evaluation and elimination of risks it will be necessary to assess the risks that remain, work on strategies to minimise these risks and to train employees in the new work methods that have been developed as a result.

It should be noted that health and safety measures must include not only assessment and management of risks but also provision of first aid equipment and procedures plus training in health and safety matters. As a minimum in terms of first aid provision an employer should provide a well-stocked first aid box (appropriate to the workplace) and an appointed first aider who has received the relevant training.

Training in health and safety matters should be put in place throughout the organisation. Some of these needs can be met through formal, external courses, in-house training and informal newsletters and meetings. The following members of staff will all need training in health and safety matters to some extent.

The manager (or owner of a business)

The person in charge of health and safety policy and procedures will need to understand the organisation's legal obligations and also the specific risks that exist within the workplace and how to deal with them.

Senior managers

Senior managers (even those with no direct responsibility for health and safety) have an important part to play. They have to ensure that health and safety is given the importance it demands in any business and, as we said before, they can do this by showing personal commitment and also by ensuring that it is given the same priority as any other area of management.

Supervisors

Supervisors and anyone with responsibility for other members of staff need to understand the organisation's health and safety policy and be able to implement it properly. They will also need to be trained in the specific risks that have been identified in their work area and in how to manage those risks.

Designated first aiders

People who have been designated as first aiders will need training. Part-time courses in basic first aid that comply with HSE are available at local colleges. These first aid skills must be updated periodically.

New employees

Health and safety should certainly be part of the induction training of all new members of staff and also for anyone who changes jobs. At the very least, new employees must be informed about safety procedures such as emergency drills, first aid and so on. They may also need training in the management of risks in their new work area.

All employees

Everyone at work needs to understand their organisation's health and safety policy and also how to work safely and without risk to themselves and others. Part of the training should cover how they can play a part in keeping risks to a minimum and creating a safe work environment, and also how to report hazards.

The Health and Safety at Work Act 1974 requires employers to provide the information, instruction and training that is necessary to ensure, so far as is reasonably practicable, the health and safety at work of employees. This training must be provided during working hours and at the employer's (rather than the employee's) expense.

Case study

Bill, the owner and manager of an electrical repair business and shop supplying spare parts for household electrical equipment, implemented a fire safety policy. First he assessed the risks, which he found included trip hazards, manual handling and risks associated with the use of electricity. He also realised that despite the risk of fire associated with the work done he had not developed a formal fire safety policy. He set out the fire procedure in a booklet he gave to all employees. This included instructions about where to congregate in the event of a fire and specifically gave responsibility to some employees for escorting any customers out of the building. He installed fire alarms and extinguishers and set up a regular programme of testing of these plus the few electrical items they had in the staff canteen. He also appointed a fire warden (with himself as deputy) who was responsible for the evacuation procedure and for monitoring the risks and procedures on a regular basis.

Bill commented, 'This is something I should have done much sooner. It didn't cost much but I feel much more prepared and safer now. I have minimised the risk to my staff and to my business.'

In the next section in this chapter about health and safety, we will look at monitoring the systems that have been put in place.

Monitoring the systems

In order to ensure that the health and safety systems that have been put in place achieve their objectives it is necessary to monitor activities carefully. Reports should be produced in two ways:

1. As a matter of routine – information about checks that have been carried out, sickness absence, maintenance programmes, training that has taken place and so on.
2. When an incident takes place – some incidents, for example accidents, will be reported immediately they have taken place and an investigation may be carried out as a result.

The result of these reports, if used correctly and appropriate action taken, will show benefits for the organisations such as:

- reduced sickness absence
- a reduction in injuries
- a reduction in the number of working days lost as a result of accidents
- information gathered as a result of health and safety monitoring can be used to benchmark the organisation's performance against similar organisations
- the production of regular reports and maintaining a discipline of collating information about incidents will result in a greater awareness of health and safety in the workplace.

When designing monitoring systems, including a system of reporting health and safety matters, it is always useful to incorporate, right from the start, mechanisms to put corrective action into place.

Regular meetings can be held to discuss and evaluate the effect of the health and safety systems that have been put in place.

Case study

When a new senior manager joined a medium-sized manufacturer of soft furnishings she quickly realised that the attitude throughout the organisation towards health and safety in the workplace was dismissive. She conducted an evaluation of the situation and found that the lack of attention to health and safety had resulted in higher than average accident rates and a tendency to ignore potential hazards.

She presented her findings to the board of directors and they decided:

- to appoint her as the Health and Safety Champion for the organisation
- to arrange health and safety awareness training at all levels, starting with all board members
- to devise a new mission statement for the organisation making health and safety a central issue
- to set up a group of high-profile employees within the organisation who would be responsible for the enforcement of existing monitoring policies as these had fallen into disuse
- to launch a campaign to publicise the new attitudes throughout the company
- that the health and safety group would meet on a monthly basis to discuss and monitor all health and safety matters.

The extra monitoring that was carried out highlighted the improvements that were necessary and these were carried out as a matter of routine. At the end of the first year after implementation of these measures, new figures were produced that showed several benefits to the organisation and its workers including a 15 per cent reduction in sickness absence and a 12 per cent reduction in workplace accidents. Furthermore, a survey conducted among the staff at all levels showed a greater awareness of the importance of health and safety in the workplace and also evidence of improved morale among production staff.

The higher profile given to health and safety had resulted in it becoming part of the culture of the organisation, led by the board.

The final step in dealing with health and safety is to review the approach that has been taken and this is covered in the next section.

Reviewing your approach

The main ways to review the effectiveness of an organisation's approach to health and safety are:

- Keep track of accidents – it should be a specific person's responsibility to keep records relating to accidents in each department, to analyse the possible causes of accidents, to spot trends, and to report to senior management.
- React promptly to accident reports – knowing about an accident is not enough. It is necessary to take action to help to ensure that something similar does not happen again.
- Plan a regular programme of health and safety activities – this includes risk assessments, health and safety meetings, safety inspections and communications. This will not only help to reduce risks and avoid accidents but will also ensure that health and safety matters are given prominence within the organisation.
- Organise regular meetings to review progress and revise the policy where necessary.

Paying continual attention to health and safety matters will be of benefit to an organisation as accidents (and the attendant costs and problems) will be reduced and legal obligations will be met.

SUMMARY

This chapter looked at health and safety and at meeting the legal requirements that exist to protect employees, members of the public and the organisation itself.

We examined how an organisation's approach to health and safety can ensure that it is run efficiently without endangering anyone involved with the organisation and that health and safety is not just paid lip service.

We went on to note the legislation that governs health and safety and the obligation put upon organisations such as creating a written health and safety policy (a legal requirement if there are more than five employees), carrying out risk assessments and making safety arrangements known to all employees.

We looked in detail at how hazards and risks can be evaluated using a number of measures such as accident reports, safety audits and inspections to highlight varied risks including slips and trips and those arising from the use of hazardous substances, machinery, ladders and so on.

Ways of eliminating or reducing risks were examined next including planned maintenance, safe systems of work, training and communication with employees. We saw that everyone in an organisation – or who comes into contact with it – can play their part in ensuring a safe working environment.

Regular monitoring of health and safety systems and reviewing the approach taken is also necessary.

ACTION CHECKLIST

1. What part do you play in your organisation's health and safety approach?
2. How do you think the approach could be improved?
3. Are you aware of which legislation applies to your organisation?
4. Consider and list the risks that exist in your immediate working environment.
5. Could any of these risks and hazards be controlled further or eliminated?

05

How can you manage physical resources?

Physical resources include all the following that are used in an organisation:

- Materials – anything used in the production of goods or provision of a service including raw materials (components and so on), office requirements (copy paper, pens, etc.) and any other consumables used in the business.
- Equipment – machinery, computers, conveyor belts, fork lift trucks. (These could be owned by the organisation or acquired under a lease agreement.)
- Premises – any offices and works buildings whether all in one location or in a variety of places or countries.
- Vehicles – both for personnel to use to carry out their jobs and also for deliveries.
- Energy – any gas, electricity or other source of power that is used within an organisation to power machines, heating, lighting, etc.
- Services – any services that are acquired for use within the business are considered a physical

resource. This could include logistics services, provision of canteen facilities, printing and servicing of machinery and vehicles.

The need for all of these resources will have to be assessed and then the resources acquired and used as effectively and efficiently as possible. This will have enormous implications for both the performance of the organisation and also its effect on the environment, so resources must be carefully managed. This requires a systematic approach to purchasing and managing resources to avoid overuse and waste and to ensure that essential supplies are always available. The use and control of physical resources can be taken step by step as we will see in the following sections of this chapter.

Identifying the necessary resources

The first step in making the use of physical resources more efficient within an organisation is to identify exactly what is necessary in terms of resources in order to achieve the organisation's aims. Its vision and values will also have to be taken into account. This means, for example, that if a company has stated in its mission statement that one of its most important values is sustainability and it is committed to caring for the environment then efficient use of resources such as water and power will be particularly important and all purchases will need to be reviewed taking into consideration the effect on the environment.

A list of all physical resources used in the organisation should be compiled based on planned activities and then the data analysed. There are several ways of tackling this:

- By department – get a list of everything used within a department or function within the organisation.
- Start from the purchasing department – everything they buy will need to be on the list of physical resources and this list must go back some time so that everything – even things that are only bought every few years (e.g. machinery) – is taken into account.
- Take an accountant's view – this will take in everything that is paid for and also things – such as premises – that are considered assets of the organisation.

Whatever approach is taken to this exercise it is important that the list is comprehensive.

The next step is to analyse this list to enable effective planning of the use of resources to be carried out. The following should be considered:

- Quantities used – can the quantities be reduced in any areas? Are the quantities of all items that are kept in stock correct considering the amounts used?
- Duplications – are any of the resources used by more than one department but purchased separately? If so, could the orders be amalgamated to get a better deal?
- Suppliers – do you have too many causing confusion and perhaps not resulting in the best deal? Or are you relying on just one supplier for an important resource, without a back-up plan if this supplier lets you down? Have you identified the very best supplier of the resource required? This will not necessarily be the cheapest quote received as reliability, quality and sustainability will need to be taken into account.
- Environmental efficiency – reducing an organisation's use of energy and improving how it deals with waste will manage the environmental impact of its use of resources. This can reduce costs and produce an important benefit

for the environment that can be publicised, giving an organisation an improved reputation.

● Sustainability – an organisation should ensure the responsible use of natural resources, so examining its use of raw materials, machinery and energy will improve its performance in this area.

● Safety – in pursuing a cost reduction policy in the use of physical resources it is important that safety is not compromised.

The analysis should address all of the above and evaluate how resources have been used. This examination of current usage will give a baseline from which to work towards improvements. It is necessary also to look at how this usage has changed over time so that trends can be spotted that should be taken into account in future plans. At this point it is also useful to evaluate changes that may occur both inside and outside of the organisation that may affect future use of resources. Developments such as planned expansion within the organisation or changes in the market for the products or services produced by the organisation can obviously affect future demand.

Having analysed just what physical resources the organisation is currently using, analysed trends and considered future developments that may affect resource requirements, you will need to create a plan detailing how the organisation will use physical resources.

A further aspect of this examination of the organisation's needs for physical resources should be a cost-benefits analysis. This is a process of comparing the total cost of a proposed action with the total benefit that will be gained as a result of taking the action. This will allow a decision to be made that is judged to be the most profitable.

Planning the use of resources

It is essential that a comprehensive plan is drawn up, using the analysis of the use of physical resources, to ensure that adequate supplies of all resources are available to all areas of the business while making reductions wherever possible. If a department has been given targets to meet, there should be sufficient resources of all types to enable that department to meet them. Wherever possible the cost of any planned increases in resources such as machinery, energy, materials and so on should be met from generating extra revenue from the activities of that department. So, simply producing more goods to sell is not sufficient reason to increase the resources necessary – there must be a corresponding increase in revenue and/or profits to justify the increased resources. It can be seen therefore that planning to use resources effectively and efficiently will cover a great deal of ground. The plan should include:

- estimated quantities required
- a breakdown of costs
- return on capital employed
- an assessment of the risks involved
- details of suppliers – and checks to ensure they have supplies available when they will be required
- an assessment of the impact that the proposed use of resources will have on the environment
- a monitoring plan
- a contingency plan – including actions that can be taken if the plan needs to change, e.g. alternative suppliers, how changes can be made to activities and so on.

Whether planning the use of resources in a small business, for a department in an organisation or for an entire large company, it is vital that others are involved. People who use the resources in question should be encouraged to give their views on how essential – or not – the resource is, how its use could be improved and how reductions can be made. If this is done, there will be several benefits:

- Ownership – the people using the resources will own the problem of reducing the use of resources and of using them to best effect.
- Information and understanding – by having input into what resources are needed and how they are used and by assisting in the compilation of data, workers in the affected department will acquire knowledge and an understanding of the problems faced by management.
- Monitoring – again, people involved in decisions about physical resources will be well placed to assist in the monitoring of the use of resources.
- Improved motivation – being involved will almost always help to make employees feel valued and increase their feelings of well-being. This will have corresponding improvements in performance and a decrease in absenteeism in addition to assisting in staff retention and recruitment.

Case study

Effective planning of the use of transport helped to make a major improvement in the transport costs of a company supplying stationery nationwide.

Starting with an analysis of current transport arrangements, the managing director of this small firm arranged for the preparation of a plan to reduce transport costs throughout the organisation. This analysis included every type of transport used – company cars, delivery vehicles, couriers, payments made to employees for using their own cars and all the costs associated with transport including parking, staff reimbursements, fuel and maintenance.

'At this point I realised that the costs needed to be cut significantly and started with the obvious cuts such as staff using trains instead of cars for longer journeys, but knew that more creative solutions would have to be found.'

The final package of measures reduced transport costs by more than 15 per cent and included the following:

- All employees were instructed to use trains for journeys between the organisation's two offices whenever they were travelling alone.
- Where possible journeys between the two offices to be shared.
- The interest rate for loans to employees for season tickets was increased.
- A new contract was negotiated with the company carrying out the majority of the firm's deliveries.
- Discounts were offered to customers who could collect their own orders.
- A 'Cycle to Work' scheme was set up resulting in better 'green credentials' for the organisation and a reduction in parking provision.
- Expenses were reimbursed to staff only when they used the cheapest form of transport available.
- The company invested in video conferencing equipment to reduce the need to travel to meetings and resulting in reduced costs.
- As company vehicles were replaced, more fuel-efficient models were to be purchased.

Said the MD, 'There was some resistance to change at first but within a couple of months everyone had become used to the new ways and many were actively looking for ways to save money on transport.'

Making a business case for resources

The two most important aspects of the business case for the use of physical resources within an organisation are evidence and costs.

1. Evidence – it is vital to show that a full evaluation of the need for the resources in question has been carried out. This evidence must include quantities that it is planned to use and show exactly where and how the resources will be used. Many stakeholders will want to see an environmental impact assessment being used in making a business case for the use of physical resources – especially in respect of the use of energy or water.
2. Costs – quantifying the expenditure that is deemed necessary and any savings that have been identified will mean that the people to whom the case is being made will have all they need to make a decision as to whether the case is a reasonable one and also whether it is affordable for the organisation.

Any business case for the allocation of resources should be detailed and should clearly identify the benefits to the people responsible for deciding on such expenditure.

Following the decision on the allocation of resources it may be necessary to adjust plans for the future to take account of any shortfall that may occur. For this reason it is always advisable to make contingency plans in advance.

Ensuring the availability of physical resources

The management of availability of resources is a wide ranging – and often technical – subject, the greater detail of which is outside the scope of this book. However, making sure that resources are available when required is often part of a departmental manager's role and can be accomplished on this level using the estimates of future requirements prepared during the analysis and planning stages. Having decided how much of a resource is needed and when it needs to be made available, the main task will be to ensure that suppliers provide the resources when required. This will be particularly apt in the case of materials to be used in production. The consequences of a lack of availability of, for example, components on a production line are enormous. Following these steps will help to ensure that supplies are available as and when required:

- Choose the right supplier – checking the supplier's reputation and adherence to quality standards will help. See Chapter 10 for more details on working with suppliers.
- Set up a schedule of requirements and agree this with suppliers.
- Monitor any supply contract – again, there is more about service level agreements in Chapter 10.
- Maintain a good relationship with suppliers – encourage them to report if problems occur.
- Manage stock carefully – set minimum stock levels and have regular reviews.
- Use stock in rotation, i.e. using the oldest stock first, to avoid stock becoming old and deteriorating.
- Monitor the use of all stock items – with particular emphasis on important items that would affect production.

With carefully managed stock control and good relationships with the right suppliers it is possible to keep the minimum of stock while still ensuring sufficient supplies to keep production lines adequately supplied. In effect, your suppliers become your store room for the resources you need. Although this has the obvious advantages of your not having to pay for the items until required and saving the space needed to store product, the success of this depends on three things:

1. Your supplier's efficiency and responsiveness.
2. The accuracy of your planning.
3. Your production requirements being predictable – a sudden surge in orders for a particular product could leave you needing stock that is not there.

The alternative to this 'just in time' way of stock control is to build a buffer stock held within the organisation. This will mean that sudden increases in demand can be dealt with but also means that large amounts of stock may be held that have been paid for but are not required for some time.

Keeping stock in hand to meet most eventualities or using suppliers as stock holders are the two main considerations in stock control for items required for raw materials and production components but other things must be taken into account when items are held for other purposes, for example consumables such as fuel (petrol, oil or solid fuel), office supplies and so on. In the case of consumables the following might be considerations:

● Usage patterns – usage of some items may be lower at certain times. For example, fuel consumption will usually fall in the summer when many company car users may be on holiday.
● The possibility of a prices increase – do you want to buy more to delay the effect of the increase?

- The space available to store these items – if all you have is a small stationery cupboard, for example, you will not be able to buy envelopes or copier paper in bulk.
- Bulk discounts.

Whatever the type of stock, having it available when it is required and in appropriate quantities is vital to the efficient running of any organisation and this can only be managed by careful planning. Thorough analysis of the organisation's requirements will, as we have seen, be essential in this process. To further improve performance in this area continual monitoring of the stock situation will be necessary to check – and adjust where and when necessary – that the forecasts and purchasing decisions are working.

Monitoring the use of resources

The use of resources – from purchase of the resource to disposal of any waste connected with it – should be monitored continuously. Monitoring should not be viewed as a process that comes when final results are assessed and the success of any changes is evaluated, but should be something that goes on at regular intervals to check the progress towards the agreed objectives. It is important that a system and schedule for monitoring progress should be built into the plan at the initial stages. If results are not measured, especially in the early stages of the resources plan, it will be impossible to know if the organisation is on the right track and, if not, corrective measures taken. There must be specific targets set that are quantifiable so that it is clear whether or not the objectives have been met. It will then be a relatively simple task to compare data from before and after implementation.

However, monitoring progress is not simply about checking figures. It is also about people, so it is a good idea to schedule regular meetings where team members have the opportunity to update their manager about progress made and about concerns they may have about how things are going. It is also an opportunity to celebrate results achieved so far. This is all part of the process of keeping a team on track and achieving results.

Of course, if it is found that the objectives are not being met, it will be necessary to put contingency plans in place as mentioned earlier. Above all, it is vital that results are not simply measured over time and then the data that is produced and the feedback received ignored. Monitoring is only useful if action is taken in response to the results.

In the same way as the people directly involved in the use of resources in each work area should be involved in the analysis of requirements and use of resources, they should also be closely involved in the monitoring of the use of the resources. If everyone is aware of the results being produced then they will be able to react appropriately – by making changes if necessary or doing more of the same if success is being achieved.

Managing physical resources efficiently is vital to the success of any organisation. This includes the management of resources such as water, electricity and gas and an organisation's use of these resources has an important effect on the environment. This is covered in the next chapter.

SUMMARY

This chapter looked at the physical resources used in an organisation – equipment, materials, vehicles, premises and energy. The need for, and use of, all these resources must be identified and assessed to ensure they are used as effectively and efficiently as possible.

First we detailed the different ways of identifying resources including by department, from a purchasing department's point of view and by an examination of outgoings and assets. In order to provide a baseline for improvements the current use of resources should be examined to avoid duplications, over-spending and environmental problems.

Next we looked at how the use of resources can be planned for the future. This must be closely aligned to plans for the business and ensure that profitability is maintained.

Managing the availability of physical resources on a large scale is a specialist job but many managers do this on a smaller scale as part of their jobs. This requires accurate estimates of requirements and encompasses choosing the right suppliers, developing good relationships with them and close monitoring of supply contracts and stock items.

We saw that the use of all resources – from purchase to disposal of any waste – must be monitored and lessons learned. This is easier to do if the people using the resources are involved in monitoring them and in making any necessary changes.

ACTION CHECKLIST

1. Do you know exactly what resources are used in your department?
2. Could you identify any areas where wastage occurs or where the wrong item has been purchased?
3. How environmentally efficient is the purchasing operation in your organisation?
4. What, if anything, could be done to improve your organisation's use of resources such as materials, machinery and so on?
5. Are resources always available when required in your department and, if not, what could be done to improve availability without over-stocking?

06

What impact on the environment does your work have?

The work carried out by an organisation can have many effects on the environment. Some of these will be subject to legislation with which the organisation is legally bound to comply.

Assessing the impact that your organisation has is vital not only to ensure that the organisation complies with current legislation but also to be aware of possible negative impacts. It is not until the effects on the environment are fully understood by the managers of an organisation that work can begin to improve the organisation's environmental performance. As always, it is important to set objectives and for the purposes of a review of the impact on the environment these should include each of the aspects listed below.

Identification

A thorough assessment of current operations must be carried out to identify the environmental impact. This should be done in conjunction with staff in each area to be assessed and should take into account both normal operating conditions and the conditions that may apply in abnormal circumstances and emergency situations. The following issues should be included:

- the site's use of electricity, water and gas
- the raw materials that are held on site
- emissions from the site
- waste – both solid and liquid
- existing policies in operation in the organisation, for example health and safety and quality policies
- noise and vibration.

Assessing impact

Having identified the possible environmental impact areas, the next step is to assess that impact. Some will be the subject of legislation while others will be viewed as having significant impact and it will be necessary to make a detailed assessment of these areas. Aspects of each impact such as damage to natural habitats, contamination of air or water or use of resources must be assessed and noted.

Quantifying

Most areas where an environmental impact is identified will need to have that impact quantified. So, items such as emissions, use of utilities and so on will have to have figures put to them. From these it should be possible to set targets and objectives for improvement following this review.

Evaluation

During interviews with members of staff who have responsibility for production areas and so on, note should be taken of past history. Any examples reported of environmental accidents and emergency situations that have previously taken place will need evaluation.

Identifying opportunities

As the review is progressing there should be an effort made to seek out and note areas where improvements in environmental performance can be made.

When the review has been completed, it will be possible to go on to develop and implement an environmental policy for the organisation. This is the subject of the next section.

Organising your work to reduce its negative impact

Using the results of the environmental assessment an environmental policy can be set up that will reduce impact of the work of the organisation on the environment. Targets can be set to improve the organisation's environmental performance and to deal with areas of particular concern. Obviously, if specific areas have been identified that are having a significant detrimental effect on the environment then these will have to be remedied without delay.

An effective environmental policy should be kept as concise as possible and be made easy to understand by everyone. It will include:

- A statement of commitment to improved environmental performance and to complying with the relevant legislation. This should be made by senior management.
- The results of the environmental assessment carried out as described in the previous section.
- The objectives and targets that have been set to reduce the organisation's impact on the environment.
- A commitment to recycling and reuse whenever possible.
- Details of how employees will be involved and methods of communication about environmental matters.

Implementation of an environmental policy will involve extensive communication with employees to ensure that they fully appreciate the organisation's commitment and how they can play their part. Suppliers and customers should also be kept aware of how the organisation deals with environmental matters and the efforts being made to improve performance. Consider how the following methods of communication could be used to spread the word in this area to all the groups of people who need to be kept informed:

- Newsletters – these can be internal for employees or external for suppliers and customers and can be in hard copy or sent via email.
- Intranet – the organisation's internal computer system can be an ideal method of informing employees, especially if all – or at least the majority – use the system on a daily basis.
- Messages added to invoices, orders and other regular communications with people outside the organisation.
- Messages put in with employees' payslips.
- The annual report should contain a section on the organisation's approach to the environment and its performance over the previous year.
- Regular or one-off meetings to inform of major changes or to update on a regular basis.

- The organisation's website.
- Training sessions.
- Notes on packaging used for the organisation's products.

At an absolute minimum there should be targets set following the assessment of the organisation's environmental impact that will ensure that legal requirements are met. Following on from this, targets can be set that will improve the organisation's performance in areas that have been identified. This could be something as simple as reducing fuel usage by making people aware that lights should be switched off when leaving a room empty or increasing recycling of waste paper by placing special bins in offices. Having set targets for improvement, the effect can be continued and increased by reporting the results of all environmental efforts by some – or all – of the above methods of communication so that everyone is kept informed. These targets should, as always, be SMART – Specific, Measurable, Achievable, Realistic and Timely – and they should always be written down and reviewed on a regular basis. We can look briefly at how SMART targets can be set that apply to environmental improvements.

Specific

You will need a number of targets relating to environmental issues you have identified. Each target should specify just one issue rather than trying to come up with one, general target that covers everything.

Measurable

Many targets can be set as percentage reductions – for example, in energy use or emissions – but make sure that they relate to a figure that can be identified and that there can be no doubt about whether the target has been met.

Achievable

It is important for morale and clarity that any target set is seen as possible to meet in the time allotted.

Realistic

A series of targets, each one following on from the previous target once the first has been met, is preferable to just one target that seems unrealistic.

Timely

Deadlines are always necessary. A vague target of a reduction of 10 per cent in electricity use is pointless if it is open-ended, for example. Far better to give a date when performance against targets will be reviewed.

Environmental awareness and improvements should be made part of employees' job descriptions wherever possible and appropriate. It should not be one person's responsibility but should be something that is viewed as a fundamental part of working for the organisation in just the same way that reducing costs or improving profits are often stated aims in job descriptions. However, it is vital to make one person a focal point of all the efforts being made to improve environmental performance and it is often useful, especially in very large organisations, to develop a team who will carry out and oversee the duties involved, reporting into this one person. Depending on the size and type of organisation, a number of areas will need to have staff appointed to take responsibility and to carry out the work needed to set up and operate an effective environmental management system. Consider involving or appointing the following:

- A quality assurance manager – quality and the environment are closely linked and if the existing quality management system is well developed then it will probably be similar to that needed to manage environmental matters so time and effort can be saved here.
- A site manager – any premises where people are employed will have an environmental impact and a site manager can take overall responsibility for a wide variety of environment concerns such as storage of materials, use of energy, safety matters and so on.
- An operations manager – specific production processes may require an expert view on reduction and control of their environmental impact.
- A health and safety manager – the responsibilities here will include hazardous substances and other areas that are of environmental concern.
- A purchasing manager – anyone with responsibility for purchasing materials, machinery, equipment or utilities will need to be involved in environmental policy so that the impact of any necessary changes to what the organisation uses can be evaluated and put into action.
- Employee representatives – they could be used to 'champion' the new focus and to channel employee concerns and ideas for improvements.

All of these roles will require training and all the people involved will need to attend regular meetings so that they are in a position not only to set up and run the environmental management system but also to roll out the system throughout the organisation, involving all employees.

Finally in this section, it is important to set dates for regular reviews of environmental policy to determine whether or not the policy and the targets set are still appropriate for the business and to set new targets for the forthcoming period to ensure that continual improvements in environmental performance are made. Included in this review should be a check that current environmental legislation is being adhered to as changes continually take place both in legislation and within the organisation.

INSTANT TIP

Ensure that reviews take into account not only normal operating conditions but also any extraordinary conditions that may occur. So, for example, include in the review a check of all accidents that have taken place and other unusual circumstances such as a factory shut down.

Having a positive effect on the environment

Organising the work that your organisation carries out so that it has a positive effect on the environment will have two main benefits:

1. Compliance with environmental protection legislation will be achieved.

2. It can make the organisation more competitive – if an organisation's efforts and successes in the field of environmental protection are well publicised it will be possible to attract people with similar values to the business. This could include customers, suppliers and employees.

So, what can be done on a day-to-day basis to make the activities of the organisation have a positive effect on the environment? Obviously, the first and most important step is to reduce negative impacts by implementing an environmental management policy throughout the organisation. However, there are many steps that can be taken that, although small, can have a positive impact. Consider:

Vehicles

Not all vehicles used in a business can be hybrids (although these are usually a good choice) but there are several ways that the use of vehicles for transporting people or goods and delivering services can be less harmful to the environment. Smaller or newer vehicles can use less fuel and have lower levels of emissions. A little training as to the best way to drive to reduce fuel consumption can also produce positive results in terms of fuel usage. Further savings in transport costs can be made as a result of planning business travel more efficiently, introducing incentives for staff to change behaviour, for example by car sharing or cycling to work.

Business travel

In addition to the use of company cars, many organisations spend huge amounts on business travel, often by air, which has a detrimental effect on the environment. Having a policy of flying only when absolutely necessary, using trains when possible and using video conferencing (or telephone calls) instead of face-to-face meetings with other members of the organisation and keeping visits to export customers to a minimum, will reduce costs to both the organisation and to the environment.

Paper

A major source of waste in offices is paper so it is worth making an effort to reduce, reuse and recycle in this area. A number of simple steps will produce real results:

- Only print or copy letters, reports, emails, etc., if absolutely necessary.
- Use double-sided printing where possible.
- Use emails rather than 'snail mail' for letters, invoices, newsletters and any other communications with staff, customers and suppliers.
- Sign up to the Mailing Preference Service at www.mpsonline.org.uk to reduce junk mail.
- Keep careful control of stock of pre-printed marketing material, letterheads, business forms, etc.
- Reuse wherever possible – scrap pads can be produced using the other side of paper that is printed on one side (non-confidential items only) and some packaging materials can be saved and reused.
- Recycle waste paper by placing bins for collection near desks, photocopiers and in factories. Encourage staff to recycle using posters and by making it easy for them to comply.

Utilities

Excessive use of electricity, gas and water by a business can affect the environment. There are several ways to control this usage such as lowering the temperature of water used in manufacturing processes or the thermostat settings in staff areas (although care should be taken to comply with regulations regarding minimum working temperatures), switching lights off when a room or site area is not in use, setting targets to reduce electricity, gas and water usage throughout the organisation or by developing an investment programme to purchase equipment that is more fuel efficient.

Helping to protect the environment by reducing consumption of water and power is central to the policies and values of most organisations but there is another important advantage of controlling usage in these areas – cost savings. For these two reasons, it is worth considering making a real effort throughout the organisation to save water, fuel and so on. The following methods will assist in this:

- Water – buy water-efficient equipment for washrooms, production processes, etc., keep a check on leaks, dripping taps, etc.
- Energy – check energy tariffs from a number of suppliers to ensure that you are being charged the most competitive rate, put in place policies that will reduce energy consumption such as instructions to switch off lights when not required, not leaving computers and other devices on standby, installing adequate insulation and buying energy efficient equipment.
- When buying new equipment take note of energy ratings – energy efficient machinery will reduce costs and help the environment.
- Ensure that all equipment is well maintained so that it works efficiently.
- Check all insulation to ensure heat is not escaping unnecessarily.

INSTANT TIP

There are legal requirements for businesses to reduce energy usage in order to meet national targets for reductions in carbon dioxide emissions so it is important to be aware of what your legal obligations are.

Drinking water

This is a very small step but it still counts. If your organisation supplies bottled drinking water for staff use and it is also laid out on the tables at meetings and training courses, savings can be made by installing a filter system to ensure drinking water from the taps is acceptable.

Houseplants

Another small step – use houseplants not only to brighten up an office or shop environment but also to remove indoor air pollutants.

Packaging

A review of the use of packaging by a manufacturing organisation can result in the identification of various areas where a more positive effect on the environment can be achieved. This includes changing from plastic bags to paper or biodegradable packaging or reducing the use of packaging wherever possible.

Supporting local businesses

All businesses purchase a wide range of products, many of which will have travelled hundreds, if not thousands of miles, before they reach the point of use. Any organisation can adopt a policy of buying local. This is especially effective when foodstuffs are considered. Taking notice of where products are produced can bring results in this area.

Protected species

Consideration of protected species will ensure that they do not become extinct. Any outside operations and building works can affect natural wildlife. There are laws regarding the protection of certain species with which all organisations must comply.

Composting

Any food waste that a business creates can be composted. This results in nutrients being returned to the earth.

This list is far from exhaustive – there are many more ways in which any organisation can act positively towards the environment and a little research in this area can produce valuable results.

INSTANT TIP

To demonstrate a commitment to the environment it is a good idea to include reference to it in the organisation's mission statement. This will reinforce the organisation's determination to improve performance in this area.

Implementing changes to work practices

With the environmental management team in place, the initial assessments carried out and targets set, it will be a major step forward to put the plans into action. Quite often there will be resistance to the changes necessary when an environmental management policy is set up. Many people may feel that they have enough to do without the extra work involved in environmental matters or they may feel that such work is not productive and adds nothing to the organisation or to their individual performance. These attitudes will usually come from a position of relative ignorance in that employees may not appreciate the benefits to an organisation of an effective environmental policy or of the necessity to meet legal requirements. The first management action in this case should therefore be to communicate with employees at all levels, making sure that everyone appreciates the importance of the issue and what will be expected of them. Newsletters or meetings can be used to communicate the legal position, the benefits for the organisation and to reassure or motivate where necessary.

The next step will be to put in place the training that will be necessary. Specific training for some or all of the different members of the environmental management team will probably be necessary plus general awareness training for everyone else. In addition, it may be helpful to consider management training for the person who has been given responsibility for implementation of the organisations' plans for environmental improvements. This could include leadership skills such as motivation, running effective meetings and so on.

Another issue to be tackled when implementing new systems such as this is the need for resources. These include, as always, financial resources, but also the time that must be made available both for people specifically involved in managing the system and also for all other employees to attend meetings and to incorporate any extra duties into their working day. In the case of the environmental management team there will be a number of extra tasks involved including arranging meetings, communicating with everyone else involved, developing and documenting new work systems and procedures, keeping track of the appropriate legislation, monitoring the system and the results it produces, updating records and targets as necessary and arranging training.

INSTANT TIP

Utilise and build on existing systems where possible. If the organisation already has a quality management system or a procedure for reporting accidents and 'near misses', it may be possible to use these by adding to them or to develop something similar for environmental management systems.

Where can you go for advice?

All organisations should be aware of their responsibilities regarding the effect on the environment. As we said earlier, there should be someone who can coordinate and lead environmental improvement efforts and it may be necessary, if there is no one appropriate for this task within the organisation, to look outside and employ an environmental consultant. A consultant can be employed to do some or all of the necessary tasks associated with an effective environmental policy including:

- Specialist advice on specific matters such as legislation and applying for the relevant permits and licences.
- The initial assessment of environmental impact.
- Developing an environmental policy.
- Setting up an in-house department to manage the environmental policy.
- Acting as the organisation's environmental manager.
- Identifying changes to work practices that would result in savings and a positive impact on the environment.
- Training requirements.
- Occasional consultancy on matters as they arise. This could include specialist advice or interim management or visits to implement changes in special circumstances such as a change in production methods.
- Auditing.
- Regular visits to check that the policy remains appropriate and effective.

Finding and selecting a consultant is a task that should be undertaken with care. As always, when considering specialist help from outside the organisation, a written brief will be useful and should set out the scope of the assistance the organisation needs. This can serve two purposes:

1. It clarifies just what the organisation needs
2. It will guide the environment consultant as to the organisation's requirements and expectations.

Checks should be carried out to ensure that the consultant:

- has relevant qualifications
- can supply references from customers (and these should be checked out)
- has relevant experience – do they understand the industry in which the organisation operates?
- can cover all your organisation's needs in terms of environmental procedures, e.g. are they experienced trainers with the relevant qualifications?
- has the capacity to cope with the work that will be generated
- has professional indemnity insurance to an appropriate level.

All of these things can usually be checked out on the internet or by asking the consultant directly. Advice about choosing any consultant is available through Trade Associations, Chambers of Commerce or Business Link offices. Also, there are a number of bodies that have extensive advice and information available. These include the Chartered Institute of Water and Environmental Management (CIWEM) and the Chartered Institute of Environmental Health (CIEH). There are also bodies dealing with specialist environmental matters such as the Association of Noise Consultants or the Energy Institute. Details of all these organisations can be found in the useful information section at the end of this book.

Being clear just what is expected at the start of any dealings with an environmental consultant will improve the outcome of that relationship. Drawing up a brief before the search begins, and then a comprehensive contract to work to, will clarify the requirements and avoid problems later on. Even where a consultant is given responsibility for all environmental matters within the organisation and has a wide-ranging brief, a senior manager will have to take responsibility for a number of areas such as:

- The amount spent – keeping a careful eye on spending is essential when employing someone outside the organisation.
- Sub-contracting – it may be acceptable within the contract for certain areas to be sub-contracted to specialists but these people may still be on the organisation's premises so care is necessary.
- Confidentiality – if any of the information that will be seen by someone outside the organisation could be viewed as commercially sensitive then the consultant should sign a confidentiality agreement before commencing work. It is a good idea to make staff aware of what work the consultant will be carrying out so that they are not given free access to all areas if that is not what was intended.
- Regular reviews – setting milestones throughout the work that a consultant is hired to do will give the senior manager responsible the opportunity to review progress. In this way any problems can be spotted as soon as possible and corrective action taken or targets revised.

Finally, although an environmental specialist will be able to help with a variety of tasks as detailed above, it should be remembered that a lot of advice and assistance in this area is available to businesses via governmental organisations.

SUMMARY

The impact that businesses have on the environment has become an important topic in recent years and this was the subject of this chapter. We saw that an awareness of environmental impact is vital for two reasons – to meet legislation and to improve the organisation's environmental performance. We detailed the steps to be taken to improve environmental performance. The first is to identify areas of environmental impact including utilities, materials, emissions, waste, noise and vibration. Next it is necessary to assess this impact and to quantify it. A full review will be necessary to do this and to identify opportunities for improvement.

Next we looked at ways to organise work to reduce its negative impact. After a full review, an environmental policy can be developed. This will set targets for improvement and set out how these can be achieved. This will, of course, need to be communicated carefully to all employees.

We then examined the ways that a positive effect on the environment can be achieved. This includes replacing older vehicles with fuel efficient ones or driving to reduce fuel consumption, planning journeys efficiently, reducing, reusing or recycling paper and other consumables, making a concerted effort to eliminate excessive use of water, gas and electricity and reducing packaging materials where possible.

Finally, we looked at how advice and assistance on environmental matters can be obtained and at the types of task that may be taken on by a specialist in this area.

ACTION CHECKLIST

1. Are you familiar with the environmental legislation that applies to your organisation? If not, clarify the situation.
2. Review the environmental impact for your department and quantify this.
3. Name three areas where your department's environmental performance could be improved.
4. How could your organisation's use of energy be reduced?
5. Are there any tasks where an environmental specialist's advice may be useful to your organisation?

07

How can you make the right decisions?

The process of decision making has been the subject of many studies and many theories have been developed about the mental and physical processes that are followed. The main point to note is that a full examination of all the options must be undertaken before the decision-making process can start. Analysing a problem and then making a decision are two separate processes and although it is not absolutely necessary for one person to carry out both, in practice this is what usually happens. Alternatively, as we will see in the next section, several people – perhaps a meeting or a committee – can be involved in the decision-making process.

There has been some debate about whether making the right decision is a result of luck or gut instinct or something that people are 'just born with'. While there will undoubtedly be people for whom decision making is easy and seems to come naturally, the majority of managers will, certainly from time to time at least, struggle with decision making. Only the most confident of people (or those who are not self-aware) will always be totally sure that they are doing the right thing. The rest of us will have self doubts and will worry that we have not properly considered all the available options. The remedy for this uncertainty is to follow a process of decision making that involves a careful analysis of the problem, coming up with as many options and solutions as possible, establishing clear objectives and then evaluating the options to arrive at a decision.

In later sections in this chapter we will look more closely at the processes involved in making the right decision.

Who should be involved in decision making?

The simple answer to the question about who should be involved in decision making is 'as many people as possible'. However, although this is a simple answer, it is complicated to put into practice. The more people who are involved in the process, the more difficult it can be to actually arrive at a decision. It is inevitable that many people examining the same information about a problem will have different views and priorities and will therefore come up with a variety of solutions and so a decision may be difficult to make. Having said that, there are two points to make in favour of involving many people in making a decision. First, that taking advantage of a multiplicity of viewpoints and experience will ensure that as many angles on the problem as possible will be covered and second, that being involved in this way makes people feel valued and that they 'own' both the problem and the solution. This will result in a far more willing approach to the work necessary to carry out the decision and a more motivated workforce.

So, how is it possible to take advantage of people's experience and to motivate a workforce by this involvement while overcoming the problems of dealing with many people's viewpoints? A large part of the success that can be achieved in a decision-making situation will depend on appointing the right person to lead the process. If many people are involved then a strong leader who will be able to lead discussion and investigations, taking care that everyone is given a chance to air their views and to contribute to the decision-making process, is vital. This person will also have to be capable of arriving at a decision that is not necessarily the one they would have arrived at if left alone to decide but must suppress their own ego to ensure that a decision is taken that reflects the majority view. There is no doubt that being involved in decision making can motivate employees so it is well worth persevering in a policy of involvement of this kind. Obviously, not all employees can take part in all the decisions made in any organisation and care must be taken to keep them informed. There will be more about how this can be done in a later section of this chapter.

In selecting the people to be involved in specific decisions, it is important to try to involve as many people as possible of those who will have to put the decision into practice and those whose working lives will be affected. So, for example, managers in an accounts department should be involved in any changes to invoicing procedures and the views of machine operators should be sought when upgrading machinery in their work area.

Having said that many people should be involved in decision-making processes, it is important that this principle is not taken so far that it becomes difficult for any decision to be taken in the organisation. Some decisions will need to be made by an individual. In general terms, simple decisions, not affecting too many people and not requiring a great deal of information to make, will best be made by just one or two people whereas more complicated decisions with far-reaching and wide-ranging effects should be made by as many people as is practicable.

Finding the right information

The first step must be to analyse the problem to be solved. Usually the problem will involve a situation where results achieved have not come up to the standards set, so a thorough analysis of the problem including the possible reasons for it is an essential part of the process in its initial stages.

It is at this point that the objectives are defined. Anyone involved in the decision-making process must be clear about what the intended outcome is. One technique that is useful in defining a problem and finding its cause is to repeatedly ask 'why?' until the cause of the problem is revealed. So, for example, if sales are declining the process might look like this:

Q Why have our sales fallen?
A One of our main customers is buying 50 per cent less than this time last year.
Q Why are they buying less?
A They are now buying more than they used to from our competitors.
Q Why are they buying from them?
A Their prices are lower.
Q Why are our prices higher?
A The products are not identical – ours are a higher specification.
Q Why can't we lower our prices?
A The raw materials are too expensive.
Q Why can't we source cheaper alternatives?
A I think we can – but we will need to check that our customer will buy all their requirements from us if we do so and can offer lower prices.

This is a simple illustration of this type of questioning. Although in real life the questions and answers will undoubtedly be more involved and the information needed to answer will be harder to find, it shows how this questioning technique leads to a possible solution to the problem. It does this by getting to the bottom of a problem and thereby makes the decision-making process easier.

When the problem has been analysed the decision maker(s) can move on to finding what the options for a solution are.

Identifying your options

Decision making involves, by definition, a number of options. It is this choosing between the possible courses of action that is at the heart of decision making. Identifying all of the possible options is therefore important before the decision can be made. Trying to make a decision without having identified all the options, and with insufficient information, will greatly increase the chances of the wrong decision being made.

One popular and generally effective technique is to brainstorm the problem. This is especially useful when a number of people are involved in the decision-making process. This can not only help to ensure that all possible solutions are considered but can also motivate teams and help them to work cohesively. The team leader will need to facilitate the process, following these steps:

1. Set an objective by defining the process and deciding on the desired outcome.
2. Collect ideas from an open meeting of the team with a set time limit and ensuring that everyone has an opportunity to contribute.
3. Organise responses – sift out duplications, clarify where necessary and arrive at a brief summary of possible solutions.

The next step is where a decision is arrived at and this decision must, as we will see in the next section, be closely related to the objectives set

Taking decisions that will ensure you meet your objectives

Carefully defined objectives are central to the decision-making process. As the saying goes 'if you don't know where you are

going, how are you going to get there?' Also, if there are a number
of objectives to be met – as there usually are – these objectives
must be prioritised. They must be placed in order of priority and
defined by answering the questions 'What would happen if we
didn't meet this objective?', 'What advantages will we gain by
meeting this objective?' and so on.

In addition to making sure that decisions are in line with agreed
objectives, the following must be considered:

- Who may be affected by the decision? It is usually
  advisable to involve those people in the decision-making
  process.
- Do you have sufficient information to make the decision?
  Is this information reliable and complete?
- Can you spot trends in the information that will help with
  the decision-making process?
- Use the information to identify the problem and all the
  aspects of it that may have a bearing on the decision.
- Identify the options available.
- Evaluate the options identified.
- Be aware of the risks involved in each of the options.
- The scope of authority – are you authorised to take this
  type of decision? Or should it be referred for approval?
- Is the decision in line with the organisation's values,
  policies and strategies?
- Timing – would a better result be possible if action was
  delayed?

If decisions take into account these aspects then they have a good
chance of being the right ones to take.

The most common – and usually most successful – way of
reaching a decision is to list the advantages and disadvantages
(also referred to as a list of pros and cons) of all the solutions being
considered. These lists must be considered with the objectives
clearly in mind following these steps:

1. Consider each of the possible options in turn. It can be helpful to use a separate sheet of paper for each idea.
2. List the advantages and disadvantages of each option in turn. Take care to consider all the implications.
3. Give a ranking to each advantage or disadvantage listed with the highest score being for those considered of great significance and the lowest score being for unimportant aspects.
4. Add up the scores for each option – the highest one should be the right solution.

Here's an example of how such an option 'scorecard' might look:

Option – to purchase a new item of equipment	
Advantages	*Score*
Increased output	10
Improved technical capabilities	6
Expand product range	7
Employee reaction to more up-to-date equipment	3
Total	**26**
Disadvantages	*Score*
Cost of purchase	9
Machine downtime	5
Training	6
Employee reaction to change	2
Total	**22**

In this example the decision was made to purchase the new equipment because of the higher score for the advantages.

The advantages of using a scorecard system like this to help with decisions – whether on strictly business decisions like the one illustrated or on more personal issues – are:

- Any number of options can be considered.
- It enables a comparison to be easily reached.
- It takes into account subjective issues, i.e. how you feel about an option, which could otherwise cloud your judgement. So, in the example above, employee reaction can be given some weight in the decision.
- An objective decision can be reached.
- A number of people can be involved in a decision made in this way.
- The right decision becomes clear simply by looking at the comparative scores.

Make sure that one of the options you consider is for no change at all if this is appropriate to the situation. Sometimes the reason for a decision being difficult to take is that the option to do nothing has not been considered. Any decision reached in this way should be one with which you feel comfortable. If you are uneasy about a decision it is advisable to check that you have included all the relevant points in your scoring and also that you have weighted the various items consistently.

There are a number of things that must be avoided if the correct decision is to be made. These include:

- Partiality.
- Over-optimism – seeing everything in a positive light and refusing to see the seriousness of a situation will lead to possible solutions being ignored.

- Inertia – unwillingness to change is a common problem but one that must be avoided in any management situation. It may be the case that what has been done before is also correct in the current situation but change should not be ruled out as this is limiting the options being considered.
- Trying to please everyone – a compromise solution may actually be the best solution but it should be reached because it is the best one, meeting the objectives and resolving the problem effectively, rather than simply pacifying people involved in the process.

Communicating your decisions

The first thing to realise when considering how and when to communicate any decision that has been made is that the way in which it is communicated is almost as important as the decision itself. If communicated badly, any decision can be seen as a backward step and, of course, a decision that is not communicated at all might just as well have not been taken. Effective communication must go alongside effective decision making.

The usual principles of good communication will apply in virtually all decisions made in any organisation, whether the decision affects matters and people inside or outside the organisation. It is always useful, when considering what information to give, to have a checklist to ensure that all the relevant details have been included.

Main points

Developing – and agreeing, where appropriate – a list of the key issues involved in a decision is vital.

It is also important, where the same decision will be communicated by a number of managers to their teams, that everyone has the same list of key points to get across.

Who needs to know?

Is this a decision that will have an effect on just a few people or many? It is vital to make sure that anyone whose work will be affected gets all the information they need about a decision. It is a false economy if, in an effort to save time, effort or expense, someone who needs to know is left out of the communication loop. This will lead to resentment and often to an adverse reaction that could impact on the outcome if anyone gets insufficient information or feels badly treated and then does not cooperate fully with what is required of them.

Who will be communicating the decision?

It may be appropriate for the person(s) who arrived at the decision to communicate the outcome but it is equally likely that there will be a number of people who will be required to get the decision out to their teams.

Means of communication

There are, of course, many ways to communicate and it is vital to use the correct medium so that the message reaches the right people in an appropriate and timely manner. In some cases, for example, an email will suffice while in others face-to-face communication is necessary. The importance and complexity of the information to be conveyed will also have a bearing on the choice of medium, as will the numbers of people involved. So, for example, while it may be best to communicate a simple message by email to everyone in an organisation, it will be far from appropriate to communicate by email if the message has a serious effect on someone's work role. This will require careful one-to-one communication giving an opportunity for questions and feedback and conveying the seriousness of the decision.

When will the decision be communicated?

Communicating a decision as soon as possible is usually the best option and it may be necessary to get the information out as and when it becomes available rather than waiting until all the details are known. Having said that, it may also be that timing is important so that a message does not get lost among a number of other communications or sent out at a time when it will not have the desired impact. For example, sending out a memo or calling a meeting to communicate an important decision when a large proportion of the intended recipients are away from the office will not ensure effective communication. In this case, if the timing cannot be changed then care should be taken to plan how and when the people who have missed the message will be informed.

Timing can also be important to ensure that everyone involved receives the information at the same time. Any number of problems can be created by communicating with one group of workers, customers or suppliers ahead of another group. Rumours will inevitably start to circulate if the decision is at all contentious or is seen to benefit one group more than another and this can cause harm to the organisation and also may compromise the chances of success that was hoped for as a result of the decision.

What will be the effects?

Careful consideration of exactly what is expected to happen as a result of a decision is vital. The predicted outcomes are usually seen as positive effects and are part of the objectives of the decision-making process but the negative results are often overlooked and are more difficult to predict or quantify. So, for example, while a decision about increasing prices to customers may have the aim of increasing profits, the 'side effects' may produce the opposite effect. Customers may decide to buy from your competitors if your price rise makes you uncompetitive. This may lead to a drop in sales, a consequent decrease in the amount of a product or service to be produced and costs may need to be revised accordingly. The cost per unit to supply the product or service may go up and profits down. It can be seen, therefore, that extensive consideration of all the effects of a decision, rather than just the desired outcome, is necessary and should form part of the decision-making process.

Why has this decision been reached?

Knowing why a particular decision has been reached will often make it far easier for people to understand and accept a decision and its consequences. It is sometimes a mystery to managers why, when they have tried to communicate a decision, the people on the receiving end do not appear to have heard the message as it was intended. This is partly because there is a lack of clarity in the message but is just as likely to be that the basic decision was delivered without giving any background to it or the reasons why it was reached. Not explaining a decision can be seen as arrogance but it is also a sign of a lack of understanding of human nature. It is necessary to develop the understanding of all those with whom we wish to communicate. With this understanding comes acceptance.

How does the decision fit in?

Decisions must be made in line with the values and strategies of the organisation and, while the connections may be obvious to the person communicating the decision, they may be far from obvious to the person receiving it. Again, this sort of detail helps in the understanding of the decision and will always lead to better communication. Knowing how the decision has been reached and how it fits in with the values and strategy will assist people in seeing the implications of the decision and how it will affect things in the long term.

How will we know that the communication has been successful?

It is not advisable to communicate a decision once and then sit back, assuming that it has been received, understood and accepted. It is necessary to put in place some sort of feedback mechanism. This should be done at the same time as deciding when and how to communicate the decision rather than waiting until the after-effects are felt. This will usually be easier to implement if the decision is delivered one-to-one or in a meeting where people will have the chance to ask questions. This will allow the people communicating the decision to clarify the message and ensure that the recipients have understood. For this reason, communicating important or involved decisions by memo, letter or email is often far from satisfactory. In this case some sort of checking procedure will have to take place. For example, team leaders could be given responsibility for fielding questions and also for asking questions of the members of their teams to ensure understanding and effective communication.

SUMMARY

In this chapter we examined the process of decision making. While as many people as possible should be involved in the process, in practice this can be difficult to carry out. It requires good leadership to make it work and avoid confusion.

We saw that making the right decision depends on having the right information and we examined one technique – repeatedly asking 'why?'– for getting to this point.

The next step is to identify the options available, using the information that has been gathered, by arranging a brainstorming session. It is important that any decisions reached meet set objectives and a system of doing this was suggested that involves listing and giving a score to all the advantages and disadvantages associated with each option related to meeting the objectives. The highest score obtained in this way will determine the decision.

Next we looked at the importance of communicating decisions where careful consideration of who it should be communicated to, and how, and of the possible effects, will increase the chances of success.

ACTION CHECKLIST

1. How many people are usually involved in decision making in your department? Do you think this works?
2. Consider a decision you have had to make recently – did you have all the information you needed?
3. For the next decision you have to make, organise a brainstorming session to assist you.
4. Review how the brainstorming session worked.
5. Consider how you will communicate the next decision you have to make.

08

How can you manage knowledge and information?

It is vital that the importance of knowledge within a business is acknowledged so that the appropriate resources can be allocated to managing it. As we will see in the next section of this chapter, the sources of knowledge within a business are many and wide ranging, and it is vital to the effective functioning of an organisation. Great efforts must therefore be made to protect, nurture and increase it. Ensuring knowledge is disseminated to the right people, at the right time and in the right way is essential and will require the use of management resources. Managing knowledge effectively can bring many benefits to an organisation including:

- Increased efficiency in the organisation – knowing what information and knowledge exists in an organisation will ensure better use of these assets.
- Improved products to offer to customers – product development often comes from knowing what the competition is doing and having knowledge of new technical developments in the market.

- Increased sales – an increase in sales can come from using market information, spotting trends and knowing your customer base.
- Improved productivity – sharing information throughout the organisation ensures better working practices are followed.
- Decreased costs – knowing what products are available and the rates currently being paid will help to ensure that the best rates can be obtained from suppliers.

Building a knowledge management strategy should therefore be high on the agenda of senior management. Giving business knowledge the importance it deserves within an organisation is often a matter of building the right culture, where knowledge and experience is valued and where management and employees gather and share knowledge on a regular basis. There will be more about this in the section about knowledge management strategy, but first we should look at just what knowledge is.

What is knowledge and why is it important?

First, it will be useful to define just what knowledge is and its importance to any business. Knowledge is vital to the effective working of any organisation and includes technical information that is contained in the production processes used, the designs of products, and financial and commercial information contained in customer records, invoices and accounts. But knowledge is more than this information that would normally be accepted as necessary to run a business. It also includes the knowledge and experience that the management and employees have that relates to the business. It is obvious that without all these sources of knowledge and information any organisation would soon be in serious difficulties.

A list of where knowledge exists and is used in an organisation would include the following areas.

Files and documents

All files and documents generated within an organisation or received by it, including files held on computers. Customer databases would fall into this category and these will obviously contain a large amount of commercially sensitive information. Not only would these records be likely to be of use to your competitors so should be protected for that reason, but also they should be viewed as an asset of the business as they could be used to increase sales in the future.

People

The people working in an organisation will possess experience and knowledge of the organisation that is valuable to the business and this needs to be protected to ensure that it is used for the good of the business and also that it is not taken to competitors if and when staff leave the organisation. Putting policies in place that will make the most of this knowledge and experience is essential. Competitors would often find such knowledge attractive so it is important to guard against poaching of staff. If staff do leave then this will invariably have an effect on a business and a way of minimising this effect is to make sure that information and knowledge is spread widely through the company rather than concentrated in one department or even in just one person. Capturing information where possible and arranging cross training will ensure that information and knowledge is maintained within an organisation.

Product designs

All work on new product designs, plus the documentation for existing designs, must be kept, as far as possible, within the organisation. This also applies to details about how services are planned and supplied. If competitors can access details of another company's product designs the competitive advantage may be lost.

Research

It may be that the organisation has simply carried out some market research or has a whole department devoted to research and development. In either case, the results of any research will have a financial cost and must be counted as knowledge existing within the organisation.

Work processes

Exactly how a product or service is produced and delivered is almost always unique to an organisation and this is knowledge that is valuable.

Business plans

The business plan, where the future aims and objectives are laid out, is an important part of the knowledge in a business. In many cases, this must be protected to ensure that competitors do not get advance warning of important innovations or shifts in the way business is done.

All this knowledge forms, in effect, the 'backbone' of an organisation and it must be managed. This includes knowing where the knowledge is stored, what protection is in place for it, who possesses it, who needs it and how that knowledge is disseminated. All organisations must have policies in place to determine how knowledge is dealt with and this forms the basis of the next section.

Building a knowledge management strategy

To be effective a knowledge management strategy must consider how knowledge is created within an organisation and also how it is used, shared and stored. This process will often entail, as previously stated, a culture shift to ensure that the importance of knowledge within the organisation is recognised and an efficient and effective strategy built.

The best way to start to create and implement a knowledge management strategy is to make sure that senior management are committed to the idea and then to designate someone as an organisation-wide knowledge manager. The next steps may include:

- reviewing current knowledge – what is already available and how is it kept?
- finding out how new ideas are generated and captured
- developing incentive schemes to encourage staff to share and contribute information and ideas
- making the benefits of good use and sharing of knowledge known to everyone within the organisation (i.e. increased sales, developing new products and so on).

At the centre of any effective knowledge management strategy must be the processes for sharing information throughout an organisation. It is often the case that knowledge is concentrated in pockets within the business. Senior management may be the only people who fully understand the objectives of a business, production employees may be the only ones who truly understand how a product is created on a day-to-day basis and long-term employees may have a wealth of experience that, while vital to the business, is under-valued or goes unnoticed. It is therefore important to recognise that nothing stays the same forever. Employees may leave, taking their knowledge and experience to another job, or they may retire or go off sick for a while, or a key employee may even die. The knowledge they had is then missing from the business and it may be only then that the importance of it is recognised. Sharing knowledge as a matter of routine can not only prevent this from becoming something that seriously affects a business when it is lost but also can enhance business performance when full use is made of ideas, knowledge and experience. There are many ways of sharing knowledge and which one is used depends on the situation at the time. These ways include:

● Capturing it then disseminating it. Existing knowledge must be discovered, quantified and then captured. This can be via intranets or by getting vital details down on paper – perhaps in the form of an instruction manual. In the next section we will look at who needs information and how to decide what information they need.
● Existing information can be shared on a routine basis. When processes are altered or new ones introduced there should be a system for ensuring that the people who need to know are kept in the picture. Making someone responsible for updating production manuals and someone else for keeping product designs documented, then ensuring that they use a set system listing who needs to know and how the new information must reach the appropriate people, is always a good idea.

- Encouraging contribution – as mentioned previously, an incentive scheme may be useful to encourage employees to contribute ideas and to add the information they have to a central knowledge bank. Again, this can be done through an organisation-wide intranet.
- Brainstorming sessions – these can be held regularly to allow employees to contribute their ideas for how their areas of the organisation work and how performance can be improved.

All of these methods will help to ensure that information is captured and that as many people as possible both contribute and receive information relevant to their work roles. This will ensure that knowledge does not become too concentrated to the detriment of an organisation. In the next section we will consider the decisions that are necessary in order to ensure that the right information goes to the right people.

Identifying what is needed and who needs it

There are a number of reasons why information and knowledge should be shared, including making sure that knowledge is not confined to just a few people and therefore wasted to some degree. Also, the greatest benefit for the organisation can be gained from that knowledge by making it available to those who can make good use of it. If knowledge is concentrated in the hands of just a few people within an organisation there is a real risk that problems will occur during an absence. This absence could be a relatively short one – say, for a holiday or an illness – or it could be protracted or even permanent if that knowledgeable member of staff decides to leave for a new job or to retire. In the case of a change of employer, the knowledge will be taken from the organisation and may be given to a competitor.

Although it is always better that knowledge is shared within an organisation, there is also a need to be selective about what information is disseminated and who receives it. If the wrong information – or too much of it – is shared it may be wasting time that could otherwise have been used for the benefit of the organisation and it could result in some members of staff feeling overloaded with information. Conversely, if too little information is disseminated, members of staff could feel that something is being kept from them and resentment can build up resulting in a less productive workforce.

Deciding what knowledge and information needs to be given out is a matter of understanding the information itself and being familiar with the capabilities and duties of all members of staff. The information can be split into two categories:

1 Existing information

Making sure that all important existing knowledge and information within an organisation is captured is essential in order to avoid the problems that would be caused by a member of staff leaving who possessed a lot of experience or knowledge – or was the only one to know how something was done for instance. This could include all sorts of information from customer contact details, to production methods, to how to operate a particular machine, to how often a machine is serviced or how bonuses are calculated.

Computers have made data capture within organisations a much easier task. Many types of information can be put into databases and this allows more effective use of the information as it can be sorted to extract reports and to spot trends. Computers are also useful to produce instruction manuals and so on that can be updated quite easily on a regular basis. The intranet is a widely used means of utilising information technology to help share information throughout an organisation and this will be discussed in more detail in the later section on communication in this chapter.

2 New information

Generating new ideas is an important way of making an organisation more forward-looking and competitive. This could include:

- ideas for new products
- ways to improve existing products and services
- spotting market trends
- changes in the market
- better ways of doing things.

Getting members of staff to generate and then share new information can be more difficult than simply capturing existing knowledge as it can take a culture shift to ensure that knowledge is valued in an organisation and that people are given encouragement and the opportunity to contribute. Holding regular meetings to brainstorm ideas for improvements is one way of encouraging participation.

Sharing the right information with the right employees can bring many benefits to an organisation including:

- increased productivity
- making staff feel more involved
- better staff retention
- better feedback from staff leading to improved decision making within the organisation
- increased profits
- improved competitiveness

- avoiding misunderstandings
- fulfilling legal requirements to inform employees, e.g. changes to conditions of employment.

Deciding who gets the information that results from decisions made within an organisation can be a difficult task but the easy way to check whether someone would benefit from knowing something is to ask 'Does this affect their work role in any way?' If the answer is 'yes' then they should be told. Obviously, as we said previously, this depends on the person making the decision about who needs to know having a good understanding of each person's work role. For this reason, the decision making should be filtered down to team leaders who can make individual decisions based on their knowledge of the work being done and how the decision affects the team members.

Having decided who gets to know which information, it is then necessary to select the correct method for its communication and to carry out the communication as effectively as possible and this is dealt with in the following sections.

Communicating knowledge and information

Effective communication is one of the most important of business skills. Done well, communication can bring many benefits to an organisation but done badly, it can bring disaster. As we saw above, selecting who gets to know which information is the first part of communication but the act of communication is equally important.

If knowledge and information that is held within an organisation is not shared it may be lost or, at the very least, the best use will not be made of it. Sharing information widely is therefore an important aspect of knowledge management.

Communication can be defined as the act of transmitting information from one person to another, but it can be more than this. It involves putting the message into the most appropriate format and ensuring that it is understood. It also involves receiving messages from others. Without effective communication skills, messages can become distorted and misunderstood so careful thought must go into the communication of any decision. It is vital that the following are avoided:

- lack of clarity
- ambiguity
- misunderstandings because of cultural issues
- incorrect assumptions – either on the part of the sender or the receiver of the communication
- incomplete information.

How information is communicated depends on the nature of the information and also on the person(s) to whom it is to be communicated. The choices to be made are detailed in the next section.

Different communication styles and media

With a decision to communicate and an agreed list of people to whom it must be communicated, the next step is to decide the way that the information will be communicated. This will depend, to a large part, on how many people the message must be given to. So, for example, it would not be possible to use face-to-face methods with thousands of people. The nature of the message must also be taken into account. For example, if the message includes news of redundancies or major job changes, the telephone would not be appropriate and if the workers are spread over a large geographical area and the message is not of great urgency or importance, then the medium of a meeting would probably not be appropriate. The following are some of the methods you can choose from:

- Face to face – with this method it is easiest to detect the recipients' reactions so ensuring the message is understood is made easier in this way.
- Letter – official information where records need to be kept can ideally be communicated in this way but it can be a bit impersonal and feedback is not easily received.
- Meeting – suitable for delivering messages to a group of people.
- Emails – many people consider emails to lack depth and subtlety but messages that are brief or are to be sent to a lot of people may be sent in this way.
- Telephone – an immediate method that is seen as not serious enough for some messages (redundancy or bereavements, for example) but has some capacity for delivering feedback during the delivery of the message.
- Team briefings – these are ideal if the information relates to something that all members of a team have in common, i.e. messages related to the team's work. They may also be useful for communicating general information about company changes, results and so on.
- Regular meetings – meetings that are held on a regular basis such as quality meetings, union meetings and so on are useful for communicating general messages.
- Intranets – these are ideal for making information available to everyone within an organisation.
- Notice boards – these can be used for routine or extraordinary information but have the disadvantage of not always being read by everyone so there is no certainty that a message has been received by all its

intended recipients. Misunderstandings can also arise when one person reads the message then passes on their understanding of it as this may be incomplete or muddled.

● Newsletters – this will depend on the frequency of the newsletters. Newsletters have the disadvantage that it is not possible to be certain that the message has been read and they are therefore more suitable for communications with employees, suppliers and customers if they are very general in content.

It is important that the correct means of communication is chosen to suit the situation. The person getting the message must be in possession of the complete and correct information and also appreciate the effect that the communication is intended to achieve.

Whatever medium is chosen to share information there should be some means of checking that the message has been received and understood. A system should therefore be in place within an organisation to ensure that any communication is two-way. People should not just be told something but should be given the opportunity to comment on the information they have received. This not only proves whether or not the information has been received correctly but also encourages feedback that may contribute extra information and ideas that can then be used within the organisation and shared with others. The way that feedback is encouraged – or demanded – depends upon the method of communication used to communicate the original message. So, for example, a meeting could have items on the agenda such as 'any other business' or 'question and answer session' or an email could ask a question that recipients must respond to (and can be chased up if no response is received).

Implementing standards to share, record and use knowledge

Part of an organisation's knowledge management strategy should comprise the standards set to share information and knowledge both internally and externally and to ensure that information is properly recorded and used. These standards will have to be precise and available to everyone involved. They must also be agreed at a senior level. If, as was suggested earlier, one person is made responsible for the collection and dissemination of knowledge throughout the organisation, then a cohesive policy can be implemented that will ensure standards are set and maintained. This policy must cover all aspects of sharing, recording and using knowledge in the organisation. We will now take these three aspects of knowledge one by one.

Sharing knowledge

There are two aims to sharing knowledge within an organisation:

1. To ensure that information is not lost when people leave the organisation or are not present – for example, when they're on holiday or take sick leave, when they retire, go on to another job or even die.
2. To make sure that the very best use is made of knowledge that exists within a business.

Information can be shared in a number of ways including by cross training (where employees learn about the work roles of people in other jobs within the organisation), regular briefings, newsletters, via the organisation's intranet and website and training initiatives that will enable employees to pass on their knowledge.

Recording knowledge

A continuing effort is required to record knowledge. It is not sufficient to capture the knowledge once and then forget about it, as existing information must be updated regularly and new knowledge added as required.

Creating a knowledge bank that saves useful information in a central location can be an ideal way to record knowledge. The main purpose of such a knowledge bank is to ensure that any valuable knowledge that exists within the organisation is not lost, but other important items that help the organisation to function can also be included. The information that it may be advisable to record in this way includes:

- instructions on how to carry out important tasks – this could include production manuals, marketing plans and so on
- customer database
- 'recipes' for manufactured items
- accounting methods
- the organisation's business plan – it's important to keep this in writing in an accessible location, with a back-up copy
- financial details, company accounts, etc.
- staff records – it's important to include details of qualifications and experience
- company policies – this may include policies and strategies that are followed in relation to health and safety, the environment, human resources and information technology
- important documents such as lease agreements, insurance certificates and so on.

Many organisations keep these sorts of information in writing but it can be even more useful if parts of it are made available via the organisation's intranet. The parts that are confidential, for example some information relating to employees, should be subject to restricted access.

NB Some information that is essential to the business must be protected. Intellectual property can also be protected and there is more information about this later in this chapter.

Using knowledge

When knowledge is effectively shared and available throughout the organisation it can be used to the greater benefit of the business. Efficient use of knowledge relies not only on the collection of information but also on it being readily available. It is also necessary for all employees to have the training they need to make the most of the information that is available to them.

Finally, in this section about implementing standards about the use of knowledge, it should be remembered that some information is confidential. While it will be necessary for employees to have the appropriate information about what is going on within the organisation and the knowledge that is part of the business, this information must not be allowed to get into the hands of competitors. It is possible – and often advisable depending on the sensitivity of the information and the industry within which the organisation operates – to put into place measures that can prevent employees from passing on confidential information. They can be made to sign confidentiality or non-disclosure agreements on joining the organisation so that they are legally prevented from passing on information and this will also reinforce the message that some of the information they may deal with in their employment is sensitive. This will protect an organisation's knowledge and information while that person is employed by the organisation but will release them from the confidentiality obligation when they leave the employment. If the work role is such that it would be advisable to prevent that employee from working in the same role for a competitor, it is possible to put clauses into the employment contract that will limit the employee's ability to work for competitors or to set up a rival business. These are restraint of trade clauses and it is advisable to get legal advice before trying to implement or enforce such an agreement.

INSTANT TIP

Employees can be encouraged to share knowledge by the use of a suggestion scheme that will give some sort of reward for valuable contributions that produce benefits for the business.

Protecting intellectual property

The term 'intellectual property' refers to something such as a design, a brand, logo or invention and it must be protected as it could be a valuable asset belonging to the organisation. There is a range of options for protecting intellectual property including patents, copyright, design right and registration and trade marks. Some of these will give automatic protection in law and others will have to be applied for. Most organisations will have something that needs protection in this way.

So, how do you know what intellectual property exists in an organisation? If there is any doubt about this, a full review should be carried out to:

- identify all intellectual property. This should be done by examining products and services offered by the organisation, design records, production processes, marketing materials. Consider where and how the intellectual property is used.

- establish what protection exists for each aspect of intellectual property owned by the organisation
- ascertain the value of all such property.

While identifying intellectual property it is important that computerised systems are examined. In recent years, with increased use of computers and of the internet, the intellectual property that an organisation has will have increased tremendously. Intellectual property in this area may include:

- domain names
- customised software
- databases that contain customer details, product specifications and so on.

Having identified all the intellectual property that exists, it will be necessary to check that it is adequately protected. The way this is done will vary according to the nature of the item and, in some cases, the automatic rights that may apply. So, for example, inventions that have been made as part of an organisation's operations can be protected by patents. These can be applied for from the Intellectual Property Office. Copyright, on the other hand, is an automatic right that applies in certain circumstances and could apply to items such as instruction manuals created within the business or to an organisation's website. Trade marks, logos and slogans may obtain some legal protection simply through continued use and establishment of an identity based on them but this can be difficult to prove if someone infringes these rights so it may be best to register them. This can again be done via the Intellectual Property Office – visit www.ipo.gov.uk where there is plenty of advice and help to protect all types of intellectual property. Three-dimensional objects have limited protection in law but these rights can be difficult to enforce so, again, it could be advisable to register the design to ensure adequate protection if someone copies a company's design.

In addition to taking measures to protect intellectual property through legal rights and processes, an organisation must take steps to protect them in practical terms. This might include getting staff to sign confidentiality agreements, taking care that documents and computer files cannot be accessed by unauthorised users or, in the case of computerised documents, ensuring that access is protected by a password system plus firewalls and other security systems to prevent accidental loss.

INSTANT TIP

It is always a good idea to keep a written record of all intellectual property and the protection that exists for it. A simple log will suffice so long as someone is given specific responsibility for its upkeep.

SUMMARY

In this chapter we considered the importance of knowledge within an organisation and how it can be managed. The advantages of effective knowledge management include increased efficiency, improved productivity through sharing information and increased sales resulting from using market information and spotting trends.

Next we looked at where knowledge exists, and is used, within an organisation. This includes the knowledge and experience of the employees, the designs and work processes that belong to an organisation and also its business plans. Managing this knowledge involves knowing where it is stored, how it is stored, how it is disseminated and how it is used. This requires a knowledge management strategy and this is what we looked at in the next section of

(Continued)

(Continued)

this chapter. This strategy must start with the commitment of senior management and have, at its centre, the processes for sharing information throughout the organisation.

As it is important not to lose or waste knowledge and information, we next examined how existing information can be captured and new knowledge can be generated. The benefits of sharing information include better staff retention, increased profitability and productivity.

Effective communication of knowledge and information is an important business skill in order to avoid misunderstanding and ambiguity. We examined different communication styles and media including face to face, by letter or email, in meetings, by telephone and via intranets, newsletters and notice boards. We also looked at the standards that can be implemented to ensure efficient sharing, recording and use of knowledge both internally and externally.

Finally, we looked at how intellectual property can be protected. The options include patents, copyright, design rights and trade mark registration.

ACTION CHECKLIST

1. How is knowledge stored in your organisation?
2. Do you think knowledge is used effectively in your department? If not, why not?
3. What improvements could be made in the use of knowledge and information in your department?
4. Consider three ways that knowledge is shared in your organisation and assess whether or not they are as effective as they could be.
5. List the intellectual property that exists in your organisation.

09

How can you support team working?

Team work is important in all but the very smallest of organisations as, when it works well, it will further the aims of the organisation. It can be defined as two or more people working together by combining their individual skills for the good of the team and the organisation rather than for the individual's objectives. An effective and successful team will achieve more by working as a team than the total of what they could achieve as lone workers.

The benefits of using teams to achieve an organisation's objectives include:

- Collaboration can produce better results in terms of product quality, productivity and adaptability to change.
- A wide variety of skills can be brought together to achieve objectives.
- Different personality types can balance and complement each other.
- Innovation is encouraged.
- Morale is boosted.
- Better staff cover during holiday periods or illness.

- It is sometimes possible to reduce workforce numbers by forming teams.

Alongside the obvious benefits of team working, there will be disadvantages and problems. For instance, if a team is working well, the different personality types will complement and balance each other but in a team with problems, these same personality types may clash. In addition, there will often be power struggles with a team. Although it is obvious that relationships within a team can have an effect on the team's performance it is not necessary to build a team where everyone is friends with everyone else. What is more important than relationships in a team is the behaviour that the whole team exhibits. As always, to change anything it will be necessary to change behaviour.

For these reasons it is essential that team working is supported. This support starts with setting up the teams by selecting the right number of members with the right blend of skills, ensuring that they are well briefed and well led and putting in place the necessary resources. So, what does a successful team need? The following are essential to effective team working.

Clear goals

As always, objectives should be set that are 'SMART' – Specific, Measurable, Achievable, Realistic and Timed. Everyone in the team should be clear about what the goals are and how they will know if they have met them. Preferably, team members should have some input into setting the goals. At the very least, they should agree to them and understand them.

A competent leader

It must be clear to team members that the person appointed as team leader was given the position because they are competent and possess good leadership skills. If there is a feeling that the team leader is pursuing their own agenda at the expense of the team's then the team will not work effectively.

The right culture

A culture within the organisation that actively supports teams, where successes are celebrated and mistakes not heavily penalised and where teams feel they have an important part to play in the organisation's success, is essential to effective team working. Encouragement and praise are just as important in a team situation as with individuals.

The right blend of skills

Getting the right blend of skills is important for any team. A team with a goal of, for example, improved sales results, would not be effective without people with specific sales skills. If all the team members were good with figures but less skilled at talking with customers, it would be unlikely that the team would meet its objectives.

Management commitment

Encouragement and recognition – when team members feel that their efforts are recognised and appreciated – are essential to effective team work. The team will be much more likely to function well when they can see that management is committed to the same goals as the team has been given.

Understanding

As stated previously, all members of the team must understand the objectives that are set. They must also understand their role in achieving that objective so, in setting up a team (or improving it if is already formed), the following role areas that exist in teams should be filled:

- Leading – people who fulfil this role will have good leadership skills including decision making, motivating and coordinating.
- Thinking – these people will be the 'ideas people' who come up with the ways that the team's objectives can be met.
- Doing – these are the people who make things happen. Once the way forward has been agreed within the group, they will get on with the tasks.
- Caring – these are the people who look after the rest of the group. They will keep it on course, sort out problems and provide research resources and so on to the other team members.

An evenly balanced blend of these types of skills will ensure that tasks can be accomplished and objectives met.

Trust

Not only must teams understand their roles and objectives and have confidence in senior management but they must also trust each other. A climate of trust can be established only when people are honest and respectful with each other.

Having established all the above requirements for effective team working it is essential to realise that teams cannot be set up and then left to get on with it. In all organisations there will always be changes. These may be changes to the priorities of the organisation caused by market changes or they may arise from changes in management. However the changes come about it is essential that the way the organisation works – including how the teams within it work – is reviewed and appropriate adjustments are made. There must be an ongoing climate of trust and support for teams to work over the long term.

Although teams are established within organisations primarily in order to get work done, there are many benefits that will come to the members of teams including the social contact that will come from being a part of a team, a lower level of stress when the responsibility for getting work done can be shared, the opportunity to learn from others and the chance to do a wider variety of tasks.

INSTANT TIP

Smaller teams tend to work best but it may be necessary, depending on the tasks to be accomplished, to develop larger teams to ensure an appropriate spread of skills. If teams get too large, however, there is a danger of factions developing that will work against the team's objectives.

Developing strategies

Strategies for both setting up teams in the workplace and also for supporting teams when they are up and running are essential in order to gain the most benefit from the work teams do and to ensure that they work correctly.

A strategy for setting up and maintaining teams should include the following aspects.

Deciding on the type of team to create

There are several types of team and it is necessary to choose the one that suits an organisation and its current situation. It may be that from time to time the choices – and the teams – will need to be reviewed taking into account the team's performance and the changes that have taken place within the organisation and in the markets in which it has to compete. For example, if a team performs badly it may be necessary to reorganise in order to change ways of working so that the team becomes more successful. Or it may be that the market for the organisation's product changes, for instance, from conventional retail outlets to sales becoming mainly internet based. Either of these changes may require teams to be reorganised to bring in different skills or to facilitate a different way of working.

Teams may be organised according to:

- Product – a team may be given responsibility for a product from start to finish, i.e. including development, launch, marketing, sales and invoicing.
- Function – this type of team may be responsible for a function – such as production, accounting or sales, for example – for a number of different products.

It should also be noted that it is possible to be a member of several different teams at the same time. So, for example, someone could work in a sales team for the majority of their time, act as a 'consultant' to other teams in the organisation regarding sales matters and may also be seconded to a team leading a business reorganisation or launching a new product.

Appointing a team leader

Team leaders can be appointed from within an existing team or can be brought in from outside the team if it can be seen that this person has skills to lead the team. It is usually necessary for the team leader to have some experience of the type of work that is done by the team. However the leader is selected, there may be a need for training. If a new team leader is appointed from within the group then they may already have sufficient training regarding leadership skills, including problem solving and coaching. With someone coming into the group to lead it, there may be a need for intensive training to bring that person up to speed on the day-to-day tasks that are carried out by the team.

The newly appointed team leader will need to exert their influence on the team and to lead it towards meeting the team's objectives and sometimes through many changes and difficult situations. Leadership skills and being able to gain the confidence of both the team and senior management will be vital to the leader's and the team's success. The following skills and attributes will also be necessary:

- experience of the tasks that the team will have to carry out
- good communication skills
- coaching skills
- ability to mentor team members

- problem solving
- decision making
- the ability to facilitate change
- a desire for continuous improvement
- a thorough understanding of how the team fits in the organisation and the contribution the team makes.

Appointing the right team leader is probably the most important aspect of setting up an effective team and must be undertaken with care. The introduction of the team leader must also be managed effectively. Being aware of possible resentments and expectations within the team and taking action to minimise adverse effects will be necessary.

An assessment of training needs

Managing a team is a skill that can be taught and nurtured so the team leader's training needs must be assessed as soon as possible and, where necessary, appropriate training undertaken immediately. Team members may also have some training needs to ensure that all the required skills are present in the team.

Communication systems and policies

It will be necessary not only to communicate with the team members themselves but also to ensure that they are equipped to communicate both within the team and with other teams that exist within the organisation. It is also important that the role of the teams and how they can work towards the organisation's objectives is properly understood. To ensure that teams are effective it is essential to set up systems that will make communication easy and to have policies in place that will ensure that the information that needs to be communicated is passed on effectively and in a timely manner. Any team that is kept in the dark about what is expected of it or feels that they are not communicated with properly will not perform effectively. See the section below for more detail of how communication can be carried out effectively.

Setting up systems for continual review

Teams cannot just be set up and left to get on with it. They must be monitored to ensure that the outcomes are those that were planned and also that the teams remain relevant and suitable for current plans and purposes. This involves setting targets and a plan for regular reviews of performance against these targets.

A strategy for supporting teams should include the following aspects.

Communication strategies

It will be necessary to consult employees and to communicate at all levels to ensure that objectives are achieved and that everyone understands what is required of them. This communication could take a variety of forms such as:

- Scheduled team briefings – these give a team leader the opportunity to update instructions to the team and get feedback.
- Extra team briefings – to get the team together when there is a particular message to be announced.
- Newsletters – it will motivate teams if news of their achievements is included.

- Company intranet.
- Notice boards.
- Suggestion schemes.
- Written communication such as emails and letters.
- Consultative groups – comprising both employees and management.
- Surveys sent to employees to get feedback.
- Suggestion schemes to ensure participation from employees.

There are many instructions, details of strategies and updates that must be communicated effectively to teams but one of the most important aspects is that of conveying ownership of a task. This task may be as simple and straightforward as a regular mail shot, for example, or as complex as ongoing responsibility for an entire product line including its development, sales and marketing. In all cases it is vital that everyone involved is clear that the team owns the task and that they are responsible for the outcome.

Objectives

Clearly set objectives and targets are essential to ensure that teams – and their leaders – know exactly what is required of them. There should always be input from the team, including the team leader, when objectives are being set. If objectives and targets are seen as things that are imposed on them then teams will rarely work as well as if the targets are seen as something they can negotiate and agree. Understanding will also be better if teams are given an opportunity to contribute to the formation of targets.

Incentive schemes

Incentives can be used to support and improve a team's performance but they must be seen to be fair to all members of the team and to include achievable targets. Incentive schemes can be used to give a team something to work towards as a team. If incentives are agreed with – or even imposed on – individual members of a team rather than with the team as a whole then this will breed resentment and may demoralise the team. If the team's results are seen as being contributed to by all members but bonuses and so on are paid only to some members then the team will be damaged.

Training

Two types of training may be necessary to ensure that teams work effectively. The first will address the balance of skills held by individuals within the team. A review of the skills of each team member will allow an assessment of whether all the relevant skills are present within the team and any gaps that are identified can be addressed. The second type of training is the team-building games and exercises that will ensure the team works well together. The correct exercises and training can improve morale, motivation and communication within the team and will ensure that the team works cohesively.

There is a variety of training solutions available including:

- Courses – for example about communication skills or understanding team work.
- Activities that could be carried out when a short space of time is available. An example of this would be a carefully timed brainstorming session to come up with ideas for a future project for the team.

- Workshops – these can be aimed at resolving a particular work-based problem or discussing something that is an issue in the workplace.
- Away days – these get the team out of the workplace and allow them to develop a better understanding of each other and how they can work together as a team. However, care must be taken to ensure that these are inclusive events, i.e. do not discriminate on any grounds such as race, gender or age.
- Corporate events – socialising with people we work with can facilitate closer working relationships. It can also be helpful to include partners and families in the invitations to such events to prevent work taking over the lives of employees by taking them away from their families. Helping employees to establish and maintain a work–life balance will pay dividends in terms of healthy, contented workers.

All of these different aspects of a team-building strategy are important and must be taken into account. Central to any successful strategy is effective communication and this will be discussed in the next section.

The importance of communication

Communication is simply the sending of a message from one person (or a number of people) to another. Good communication ensures that the message is understood and good communication is essential to any organisation. In any business there will be many people and organisations – both inside and outside of the organisation – who will be involved in communicating with the business and its employees. Internally, the list of people who may have to communicate with an organisation could include its owners, shareholders, managers, employees and trade union representatives. The list of people and organisations from outside of the organisation who will have to communicate with it could include customers, suppliers, government officers (both locally and nationally), media people (reporters, etc.), tax officers, accountants, solicitors, debt collectors and so on. Many people who are team members will have to communicate with a variety of these people and the importance of communication in teams is the focus of this section. If communication fails within a team it will usually lead to poor performance, objectives not being met and unnecessary conflict. For these reasons it is essential that everyone in any team realises the importance to the team of good communication and that there are clear, well-understood channels and systems of communication available to all members of the team.

Teams may need to communicate between themselves or someone from outside the team may need to communicate with them for the following reasons:

- To agree goals and objectives for the team.
- To inform everyone of the goals and about progress towards them.
- To share information, for example about a current project.
- To share skills and knowledge – this makes the most of the combination of skills, expertise and knowledge that will exist within the team.
- To impart decisions that have an impact on the team.

Poor communication will have a detrimental effect on the team and its performance. It will have a number of effects such as:

- Members may simply not understand what is required.
- Time and effort may be wasted following instructions that have been misunderstood.

- Without full instructions, the quality of work carried out by the team will suffer.
- Bad feeling may develop as a result of misunderstandings and this will affect how the members of the team work together.
- Deadlines will be missed.
- A lack of trust may develop – both of management and within the team.
- Some team members may do nothing if they receive an unclear message as they may find it easier to do nothing rather than work out what is required. This sort of response is common and can go unnoticed until it is too late to remedy.

To ensure effective communication within and between teams it is necessary to look at the three vital ingredients of team communication:

1. The message
2. The method
3. Team participation

Let's look at these aspects of communication in turn.

The message

In all communications, the message must be clear. Communication can only be successful when both the sender and the receiver of the message understand the same message that is being communicated. It must therefore be:

- Clear – does it convey what you want it to?
- As short as it can be. Obviously complicated messages will have to be quite lengthy but an effort to keep things

brief should be made to avoid the receiver's attention from failing. Don't go into unnecessary detail.

● Organised – set the message out in a logical way so that the receiver is led, step by step, to the point where they fully understand the message.

● Error free – mistakes will only confuse.

● Unambiguous – if it is possible to interpret the message in any other way than that intended then it is ambiguous and needs rethinking.

● Accompanied by the right body language if it is delivered face to face – an aggressive stance when delivering a sympathetic message will be confusing and will result in the message being misunderstood.

● Two-way – make sure that there is the opportunity for feedback. This will ensure that both the sender and the receiver of the message can confirm their understanding and adjust until full understanding and agreement is reached.

INSTANT TIP

Feedback can be both verbal and non-verbal. Pay attention to comments you receive when delivering a message but also take notice of other signals such as yawns and fidgeting that indicate boredom, or puzzled looks that will show a lack of understanding.

The method

Next, let's look at the way that the message is communicated – the method of communication. There are two basic ways that this will happen:

1. Verbally – this will include face-to-face communication, telephone calls, video conferencing and meetings.
2. Written – this includes letters, emails, newsletters, memos and reports.

The method of communication must be chosen to suit the message to be communicated. Many things will govern the choice of method including:

● The message – as we said, different methods suit different messages. So, for example, an email would be ideal for conveying brief details about a forthcoming meeting or a newsletter is especially suited to passing on information about company or market developments. Some information must be delivered face to face whereas some messages must be put in writing. Take one example – if someone is to be made redundant then it is far better to have this discussion face to face if possible so that any questions the receiver may have can be answered. Following that meeting, it will be necessary to advise and confirm specific details of redundancy entitlements, legal requirements and so on and these should be given in written form.

● The number of people to whom the message is to be communicated – with large groups of people it may be impossible to gather them all together for a meeting so several face-to-face meetings may be necessary or written communications of some sort may be more suitable. The logistics – and cost – of arranging such meetings may need to be taken into account and balanced against the benefit to the business of face-to-face delivery of the message.

● How much feedback is required – sometimes the message needs a response and in this case it is not ideal simply to deliver a memo to all the people involved. There is then a danger that the message will be misunderstood or ignored and management will not gain the feedback they need to complete the task. This will also mean that extra work will be involved in chasing up the responses and this extra work could be avoided by choosing a face-to-face method of delivering the message and getting responses at the time of delivery.

- The location of the people to whom the message is to be communicated – if the receivers of the message are all in one office or factory, for example, then it will be relatively easy to gather them together in one meeting place and deliver the message face to face whereas if they include virtual workers who may be travelling around to do their jobs or working from home then it will be far more difficult. In this case, unless the numbers involved are huge, a video conference may suit the purpose.

- The urgency with which the message needs to be treated. For example, if some urgent news about a problem must be communicated there is little point preparing and delivering a memo that may take a day or two to reach members of staff involved. Far better, in this case to hit the phones and make sure that everyone affected is kept in the picture and can then take remedial action without delay.

Team participation

Having done everything possible to ensure that the message is clear, it will then be necessary to check that it has been received and understood.

Clear messages and utilising the right communication method go a long way towards ensuring effective communication but if the message is not fully understood these efforts will be wasted. It is usually necessary therefore to monitor the effectiveness of communication within a team. This can be simple to do and should form part of every team leader's regular checks. This process can be kept simple. Consider the following checks that can be made on a regular basis and points to note when delivering a message to a team:

- Get feedback from all team members.
- Encourage all team members to contribute to discussions.
- Simply ask – by asking what the recipients need to do in response to your message, it will be possible to gauge whether or not they have understood it.
- Ask if there are any questions or concerns.
- Ask for comments – if this is met with silence it may be necessary to ask more searching questions to ensure that common understanding has been reached.
- A survey to gain opinions and comments following a major announcement to staff, customers or suppliers can be useful in determining both the level of understanding and concurrence with the message.
- Summarise the main points of the message and also consider handing out a brief, written summary for people to take away with them.
- When responding to someone's question about the message you have just delivered, repeat their question to make sure you have understood it correctly.
- Try to make sure that everyone in the team gets a chance to speak or respond in some way.
- Don't interrupt anyone when they're making a point. If you do have to cut someone short because of lack of time, let them know that you will get back to them after the meeting or when it will be more convenient.
- Keep calm – even if someone disagrees with you, it is not usually personal.

With just a few exceptions – notices, safety warnings and the like – most communication is two-way and so a message that is sent out by whatever means may require some sort of response. For this reason everyone in a team will need to have good communication skills and it will be worthwhile for most organisations to provide some training in this vital skill.

The essential tools for effective team working

Most activities to improve performance in many organisations are focused on individual workers and they are encouraged to work towards promotion and their goals for individual gain. Appraisals aim to analyse and improve what an individual employee can achieve, targets are set for individuals, bonuses are geared to individual performance and individuals work hard to gain promotion. For example, many organisations run an 'employee of the month' competition with recognition and rewards geared to the individual. All of these are tools and strategies that will enhance performance within the organisation but, by improving teams in addition to individuals, more can be done. Using tools such as the following, which create a culture within the organisation that fosters effective team work, results can be improved even further.

Culture

It is essential to create a culture within the organisation that puts team work at the forefront of its aims and strategies. Team members must fully understand their roles in the team and the part they play in creating success for the organisation. To assist with this the team leader and senior management should facilitate meetings where team members can be helped to understand where their team fits in the organisation and can see clearly how their work aids progress towards the organisation's goals and objectives. They should take part in agreeing how the team can further the organisation's vision and values so that everyone understands what needs to be done to achieve overall objectives.

Team building

Having ensured that the team members have understood the team's importance to the success of the organisation, the team leader and management must then focus on building a team that will be cohesive and achieve the desired results by working cooperatively and efficiently.

There are many activities that can help with this. These can take the form of:

- away days
- social activities
- seminars
- team-building games.

Although team-building activities such as these can produce advantages such as letting team members get to know one another better, giving the team members a common experience that can generate closeness and improving morale, these effects may only be of a very temporary nature. To ensure that the positive effects of team-building activities are continued after the activity is over they must be carefully planned and activities also arranged that will ensure a follow-up when the team is back in the workplace.

The most effective way of ensuring that team-building activities that take teams away from the workplace have real, continuing, benefits is to link the activity to work goals and objectives. So, for example, an away day could have plenty of relaxation and 'getting to know you' activities but should also incorporate sessions of planning related to real work goals. Giving the team time away from the workplace to think about what they need to do, as a team, to achieve their objectives will produce better results than any amount of sports events, ice breakers or spa treatments.

Involvement

Getting every single member of a team fully involved in the work that is to be done is not an easy task for a team leader. There will inevitably be some team members who would prefer to work alone or who do not see the benefit to themselves or to the organisation of working as a team. People will therefore need to be encouraged to take part in joint decisions and to contribute their ideas. This can be a matter of training for the team members and also of setting up systems that will create the right environment. This includes brainstorming sessions where everyone is given an opportunity to give their suggestions as to how to solve a problem or regular meetings where people are given specific roles to play. The job of chairing the meeting could be rotated, for example, or everyone given a slot at the meeting when they need to express their views on work being done by the team. Communication will, as always, play an important part in this sort of exercise. Being clear about the aims of the exercise and making sure that everyone knows and understands thoroughly what is expected of them will ensure a greater degree of success.

Empowerment

If members of a team feel that, as a team, they can control their performance, their environment and how they work towards a common goal, then they will achieve far more than if they are simply directed as to what they must do. Systems can be set up – perhaps involving a regular meeting – to empower them to make joint decisions as to how they will proceed as a team in any situation that arises. This will improve both their confidence and their performance.

Training

Teams can be trained to work together for the common good. This will involve sessions aimed at making expectations clear. All members of any team should understand what sort of team they belong to and how its work contributes to the organisation's goals. They should appreciate how they can work together, be accountable to each other and be more productive as a team than they would be as individuals.

Incentives

Incentives – bonuses, pay rises, recognition and so on – can be aimed at teams rather than at individuals and this will encourage team working and improve performance of the team as a whole. It will give the team a common goal to ensure that all members of a team are working with the same aim rather than for individual recognition.

All of these tools will help to build an effective team and help to improve both the results that the team achieves for the organisation and also the level of satisfaction within the team.

The effect of virtual working

Virtual working can be defined as working while not based in an office or other such workplace. Such working is facilitated by web technology and can provide a variety of benefits both to the employees involved and to the employer. These include:

- Lower costs for employers in relation to office space and also add-ons such as canteen facilities, on-site car parking and so on.
- It can be easier to recruit virtual employees.
- Greater personal flexibility for workers.
- Greater flexibility for employers, e.g. where their workers are situated.
- Hours of work can be spread out to cover different time zones allowing other areas of the world to be serviced effectively.

Virtual teams are simply a group of people who work as a team but who are not based in the same location and who use emails, intranets, the internet and telephones to communicate rather than carrying out their roles face to face. There are several scenarios where this may prove to be the best way of working:

- A team of people all working from their own homes.
- One or more members of a team working in each of a number of the organisation's premises – perhaps in different regions or even different countries.
- Some workers in a team may be mobile (e.g. working outside the office environment, perhaps visiting customers' premises in a sales or service capacity) or work from home while others are office- or factory-based.

Although such teams will not have their workplace in common, they will have common goals and will need to cooperate in just the same way as teams who are all based in the same premises. However, sometimes different issues are raised by virtual working and there are advantages and disadvantages of this way of working in teams. These include the following examples.

Technology

The virtual team is highly dependent on technology – computers, the internet, emails, telephones and so on – and this might be seen as a disadvantage. However, most areas of work in the twenty-first century rely heavily on technology so virtual working should not be ruled out simply for this reason. In fact, many virtual teams find that they form relationships more easily when they are linked '24/7' by the technology.

Isolation

This can cause problems for both employers and employees. From an employer's perspective there is the fear that an employee who is not working on site will not be working as hard as those employees who can be more easily supervised and directed. Of course, the answer to this problem is to choose employees who can be trusted to work responsibly whether they are closely supervised or not.

The problem of isolation for the employees themselves is that they can feel that they do not have a ready source of help and support. Most employees who work from home or whose work takes them away from the organisation's base will be people who can work independently for much of the time but even the most self-reliant of employees will need support from time to time. It is therefore vital that support systems are put in place from the start. These could include video conferencing, regular meetings with the virtual working team's supervisor and/or other members of the team, newsletters (it's important not to forget to include people who are not office based when sending out communications such as newsletters, policy updates and invitations to social events) and simple telephone calls to check everything is going well.

Communication

The most important aspect to be noted regarding communication with virtual teams is that they must not be forgotten. The amount of communication they receive should be at least as much as that directed at in-house employees. So, for example, if all employees who work at the head office of an organisation are sent a note about staff benefits or a new staff appointment or vacancy then all off-site workers should be sent one too. In addition, the additional communication requirements for virtual teams must also be noted and acted upon. Therefore the means by which they receive any information may be different, for example, someone working on site may be invited to a meeting about pension changes whereas someone who works off site may need to be informed by email with a response invited by the same method plus the offer made for them to discuss any matters arising.

The person responsible for the results achieved by any virtual team should ensure that communication systems are set up and that they are being used effectively. This will involve keeping a constant check on the technology that facilitates the communications and also on the feedback received both from the team members and from others who deal with them.

Accountability

This is related to the idea that 'out of sight is out of mind'. Many employers are initially uncomfortable with virtual working but trust must be developed. The most important aspect of this is to set up a goal-oriented culture. With clear goals and a system of measuring outcomes, any team, whether working on site or off, can be made to be fully accountable.

All of these issues can be overcome and the benefits to everyone concerned with virtual working can be realised. It is most important to deal with the issues as they arise and to set up the necessary systems to ensure efficient working.

SUMMARY

In this chapter about team work we looked first at the benefits that team work can produce. These include the bringing together of a variety of skills, encouragement of innovation, improved morale, better staff cover and the collaboration that can produce improvements in productivity and adaptability.

Next we looked at the essentials of effective team working. These are clear, agreed goals that every member of the team understands, a competent leader, a culture that is supportive of teams, the right blend of skills in the team and management commitment to team working. Within the team there should be trust and an understanding of roles and objectives.

We saw that a strategy for setting up and maintaining teams should include a clear decision as to the type and purpose of the team, the appointment of the right team leader and putting in place adequate training and a system of continual review.

Teams can be supported by communication systems and policies, clear objectives, incentive schemes and appropriate training. As communication is such an important part of team work, we looked at this subject in some detail in this chapter. This covered the three vital ingredients of team communication:

1. The message – this must be clear, concise and two-way.
2. The method – this can be verbal or written and must be chosen to suit the message, the circumstances and the recipient.
3. Team involvement – everyone must play their part in a team for it to be successful.

Next we looked at the tools that can be used to improve teams. These included culture changes, team-building activities, getting every member of a team involved, empowering teams, training and team incentives.

Finally, we examined virtual working. The areas that need particular attention with respect to virtual working include the technology used, possible isolation, communication issues and accountability.

ACTION CHECKLIST

1. What benefits do you think your organisation gains from team work?
2. Consider any team of which you are a member – do you have clear objectives and is everyone in the team aware of them?
3. Does the culture of your organisation support team working?
4. List three ways in which your organisation supports team working.
5. Think about the people in your organisation who are not based at the organisation's premises – do they have any particular problems caused by virtual working?

10

How can you find the right suppliers?

Finding the right suppliers to suit an organisation and its specific requirements at any point in time involves far more than simply selecting the supplier offering the lowest prices. In addition, it must be noted that the same supplier for a particular product or service may not remain suitable for an organisation forever. An organisation's priorities and requirements may change from time to time and also the supplier may undergo changes that cause the products offered or the service they are able to deliver to be revised so that it is no longer the best choice. For these reasons, and to get the best deal for an organisation, it is essential that suppliers are chosen very carefully and that the arrangements are continually reviewed.

In selecting a supplier the following should be taken into account.

Requirements

What does the organisation need right now? What are the priorities? A full review of the organisation's requirements is essential when considering a new supplier. It is also important to be clear about the details of the product or service to be purchased – the specification, quantities, timescales and so on. Assessing these requirements is covered in more detail later in this chapter.

Quality

In most cases the quality of the purchased items will be vital. In a very competitive market it may be possible to buy exactly the same product or service for a range of prices and then choosing the lowest price (so long as the service – delivery, after-sales service and so on – is good enough) is the route to take. However, it is often a mistake to buy lower quality goods no matter what the price advantage may be as customers will judge an organisation by the quality of whatever it supplies. The quality of goods that are bought must be consistent.

Price

Price is almost always seen as a very important factor in selecting a supplier but it would be more accurate to say that, rather than price alone, value for money is essential in all cases. Value for money takes into account not just the price of the product or service that is being bought but also other factors that will be important to a buyer such as quality and service. Purchasing decisions are almost always a compromise between buying the best and the price that an organisation is willing – or can afford – to pay.

Service

Deliveries when required and as promised when the order is placed are the prime aspect of good service that will affect who an organisation will buy from. When an order is placed a supplier should be able to give a delivery promise and then stick to it. After-sales service is also important. If something goes wrong, for example not being able to meet the delivery date or the product being faulty, how does the supplier deal with the problems caused? Good communication between buyer and supplier is vital to ensure efficient service.

Security

It's useful to carry out a credit check on possible suppliers to make sure that they will be able to fulfil an order of the size you are considering and have a good chance of still being in business when delivery is scheduled to take place.

A good supplier will be reliable and will communicate regularly (without being a nuisance) to ensure that they understand the buyer's requirements.

Finding competent, competitive and reliable suppliers is not an easy task and requires careful consideration and time to research the market. Good ways of finding suppliers include:

- Recommendation – this is by far the best way of finding a reliable supplier as a recommendation from someone who has experience of dealing with a company will help to ensure good service.
- Chambers of Commerce – your local Chamber of Commerce will have a great deal of information about local companies and will keep directories that you can search to obtain details of possible suppliers.

- Directories, local press and the trade press – depending on the type of product or service required, it should be possible to source a specialised and/or local supplier from these publications.
- Exhibitions and conferences – in a specialised market, it can be useful to attend exhibitions and conferences where a large number of suppliers may be represented.
- Consultants and business advisers – if you are undergoing an improvement programme of some kind and have engaged business consultants to help, they will be an important source of recommendations for suppliers of goods and services in their area of expertise. Advisers such as accountants, bank managers and so on will also be able to pinpoint possible suppliers.

Determining your requirements

The first step in finding the right supplier must be to be clear about the organisation's requirements in terms of the specifications and quantities of product or service required.

In addition to setting out what the organisation needs to purchase, it is also important to be clear about issues surrounding purchasing. What else does the organisation need from its suppliers? This covers price and service as detailed above and also encompasses the type of company that is dealt with and how they act. So, for example, should it be a large company with all the financial security that this may entail or maybe a small company with whom a closer relationship can be built up? Or a local company that is on hand to solve any problems that may arise with the goods or services they supply or with whom you perhaps already have a relationship?

It may also be useful to consider how many suppliers it is advisable to deal with. If too many suppliers are used the purchasing power may be diluted. In this case, the buyer may not have the influence to expect favours if, for example, an urgent delivery is required. Having split their orders among a number of suppliers the organisation may be viewed as a small customer. In an ideal world, of course, all customers are valuable but the harsh reality is that the larger the orders that are placed, the more valued a customer will become. Although it is important not to depend on a single supplier of a product or service that is important to an organisation (they may become complacent or you may find that you are unable to find an alternative source of supply at short notice if necessary), the advantages that may be possible for limiting the number of suppliers dealt with include:

- orders are concentrated giving better buying power
- possibility of better prices
- better relationships
- easier to deal with just a few suppliers
- a major supplier will usually be willing to provide a credit reference if needed
- improved service from your suppliers.

It is always useful to write down a list of purchasing requirements to ensure clarity when making purchasing decisions. This list will prove useful in any negotiations.

Assessing value for money

Value for money can be defined as getting the best possible combination of whole life costs and quality. A low price does not always signal value for money (VFM) as VFM encompasses not just price but also the efficiency and effectiveness of the product or service being purchased. If a price quoted is much lower than expected it can be a sign that the goods are not exactly what you need so it is vital that with any major purchasing decision, the organisation gets value for money. So, there are three things to be achieved to ensure that an organisation gets VFM:

1. Price – the lowest price possible after taking into account the other two criteria.
2. Efficiency – how much is achieved for the price paid. You may be able to get the same product or service at a lower cost than previously.
3. Effectiveness – the impact of the product or service purchased. To ensure effectiveness of any major purchase, you should aim for an increased level of service or quality at the same price as you have paid for previous orders.

The relative importance of each of the three elements of value for money will depend on the objectives that have been set for a purchase. Continuous improvement should be aimed for in all cases but it is possible that an organisation will have got the price down as low as possible and will need to concentrate on VFM in terms of the service levels achieved, i.e. getting more for the same price.

Negotiating with suppliers

The first thing that is usually considered when preparing for negotiations with suppliers is price but, while this is often the main focus of any negotiations, it is possible to negotiate on other aspects of a contract to ensure the best deal possible. This includes delivery or payment terms and the quality or specification of the goods or services to be supplied. The aim should be to arrive at the right deal according to the priorities and requirements of the organisation and this requires a negotiating strategy.

The first thing to do is to set objectives. What do you want to achieve? Being clear about the desired outcome will ensure that nothing is forgotten in the heat of the negotiations. As always with objectives, it is essential to know where you are going or it is possible that you will never get there. It is useful to set out what you consider important and to list them in order of priority to you and your organisation. Different organisations will have different priorities and any organisation's priorities may change over time and according to the product or service being purchased. So, for example, when buying a large manufacturing machine an organisation may consider the quality of technical support to be the most important factor whereas when negotiating the annual office stationery order, price and delivery may come to the fore. In all negotiations compromise will usually be necessary so you should decide in advance what it may be possible to compromise on if necessary.

INSTANT TIP

Deciding on your deal breakers before starting to negotiate is vital. Knowing what will cause you to walk away is just as important as knowing what will signal success.

Consider the following aspects prior to negotiating the purchase of any large item.

Price

What have you paid in the past? What is your budget? What is the going rate for the item? Would the quantity you are ordering be considered a large order for the supplier with whom you are negotiating? What are the usual discounts offered for quantity or long-term commitment? Are discounts usual practice in your field?

Delivery

Decide how important prompt delivery – or staged delivery and payments, perhaps – is to your organisation. Make sure that you know exactly when goods or services are required and also the latest delivery that will be acceptable. This may be a good negotiating point if your supplier needs to fill production capacity at quiet times.

Payment terms

It may be necessary to consult with your organisation's accountant on this matter. Do not underestimate the value of extended payment terms to your organisation as they will help with cash flow. In effect, being able to make payment long after goods or services have been supplied represents a free loan and could decrease the amount your organisation has to pay in bank charges.

Product specification

Knowing the product or service that you are purchasing is of prime importance. Only with this knowledge can you be sure of getting the right deal.

Reputation

The supplier's reputation is important as it will tell you a lot about the quality of both the product and their service. Find out all you can about the organisation – do they deliver on time, are they the market leader, do they have lots of competitors, how large is the company, is it financially stable, have they plenty of orders or are they finding business tough?

Service

What is the supplier's after-sales service? Do they respond well to requests for assistance and complaints?

Other aspects

Could the deal include product training (especially useful in the case of machinery and software) or could there be any free add-ons?

INSTANT TIP

Make sure that you're negotiating with the right person(s) in your supplier's organisation. Always make sure that they have the authority to sanction maximum discounts and to make delivery promises.

Another point to consider is whether you will be negotiating alone or as part of a team. This decision could depend on how many people will be involved on the supplier's side and also on staff availability. Aim to match the supplier's team in terms of numbers, seniority and breadth of knowledge. This is important as feeling at a disadvantage for any reason is not conducive to a good result. If you are part of a large negotiating team make sure that everyone is fully aware of the negotiating strategy and of the list of priorities that has been drawn up.

All of these aspects of the purchase should be researched and decided before commencing the actual negotiations.

A last point to consider is that in any negotiations it is never a good idea to arrive at a deal that, while it may be extremely good for one side, is not comfortable for the other side. There are several disadvantages to negotiating so fiercely on price, including:

- The supplier may walk away from the negotiations.
- A reduced price may be obtained at the expense of something else that is important to you, such as quick delivery or 24-hour service call out. On a low price a supplier may have to cut his costs and therefore not provide everything to the standard you need.
- The supplier may go out of business if his margins are not high enough.
- The relationship with your supplier will suffer.

Buyers and suppliers need to form a relationship that will be a partnership and is valuable to both and this is the subject of our next section.

Establishing effective working relationships with suppliers

As we said previously, it is important not to push so hard for a low price that the deal becomes one that the supplier finds hard to live with. However, there is more to a relationship with a supplier than the negotiations. Remember that even when a price and all other conditions of sale have been agreed – and even supposing that everyone is equally happy with the deal – the order(s) must still be fulfilled. You will need to develop a working relationship with all suppliers used by your organisation and this is especially important in the case of main suppliers. There are many ways in which you can build and enhance relationships with suppliers.

Understanding

The more you understand your suppliers – their business, their problems, their people – the better the relationship will work. If you recognise their busy times and tailor your orders and other dealings with them to take account of this as far as possible, they will appreciate this and, hopefully, will return the favour with, for example, quick deliveries when you really need them. Of course, this understanding can work both ways so informing them about your business will improve the relationship too. As you can see, good relationships with suppliers are a matter of give and take.

Become important to them

Bigger customers are more important and are (usually) treated better by suppliers. Other ways to become important include helping your suppliers by being flexible, paying on time and so on. It might also be possible to get good deals or better service by agreeing to buy a product or service exclusively from them.

Meeting

Apart from noting how business is conducted on a day-to-day basis to see how it can work in everyone's interests, the main way to develop a good relationship with suppliers is to meet them, face to face – on a regular basis. Discussions can range from specific matters relating to customer service or ongoing orders to future plans for both businesses.

Be a good customer

This involves helping your supplier in a number of ways including paying promptly and discussing order fluctuations and requirements in plenty of time to allow them to react and also in ways not strictly related to your orders. This could include inviting them to events held in your organisation and introducing or recommending them to your contacts who may be potential customers for them.

Formalise agreements

A contract and service level agreement will avoid disputes about what has been agreed at the negotiating stage and will ensure that the buyer is clear about what will be supplied while the supplier knows what has to be done. In any agreement about service levels it is important to include what is expected of both the supplier and the buyer such as deadlines, payment terms, reporting procedures, the standards required and how disputes will be resolved. Some service level contracts, usually for the very largest of supply deals, will set out compensation to be paid in the event of service failures such as late delivery.

Review performance

It is a good idea to put a review system in place as soon as the contract is agreed. Matters such as delivery performance, payments and other ongoing issues should be discussed at regular intervals to ensure that what was promised – on both sides of the agreement – is what actually happens.

Ideally these reviews should be carried out at regular meetings that allow for two-way communication about how the contract is going. In addition to it being an opportunity for the buyer to assess how well delivery promises and other aspects of the purchase contract have been adhered to, it will also allow the supplier to review how the contract is being managed and that payments are being made on time. It is the ideal opportunity to further the relationship with a supplier.

Performance reviews and meetings will spot problems at an early stage before the relationship is seriously affected and will therefore help to ensure an ongoing, successful relationship in the long term.

Using a tendering process

Formal tenders are usually used for larger supply contracts and involve inviting prospective suppliers to bid against a detailed specification. Although it can entail a lot of work it can be a very useful way of deciding on the right supplier for a large contract. Tenders are usually produced by experienced buyers but occasionally managers with less specialised skills may be called upon to put together an invitation to tender. In any event, a tender must follow the organisation's procurement policies and be carefully controlled.

The first step is to draw up a specification for the products or services required. This should contain:

- a clear description of the product needed – including quantity and quality, technical specification and so on
- cost guidelines where appropriate
- time constraints – delivery requirements should be detailed.

When the product specification has been completed (and checked, if necessary, by others in the department) an invitation to tender should be prepared that details the tendering process advising prospective suppliers how to submit their bids, how these will be evaluated and the deadline for receipt of bids. It is customary to include some background information about the organisation to help prospective suppliers to decide whether to apply. If you intend to use a shortlist procedure then this should be mentioned at this stage.

Most tenders are more than just a request for prices and delivery promises. If your organisation has a large contract to award, the tender process can be used to obtain solutions to problems and for that reason prospective suppliers will usually include some creative input in their bids. For example, you may be looking to extend the life of your product in the market or to cut the number of staff required to run one aspect of the business and the tender process may help.

Invitations to tender should then be sent to prospective suppliers. These suppliers should be selected according to their suitability and the number of invitees should reflect the size of the contract and the market in which the organisation operates. Care should be taken not to invite too many bids as this will create a lot of work but, on the other hand, sufficient bids should be invited to ensure adequate coverage of the market. Many tenders are advertised in the trade press in order to encourage bids from suitable companies.

As tenders are part of a formal procedure, detailed criteria should be established that will ensure that queries from prospective suppliers are answered promptly and without bias, record receipt of bid documents and treat all participants fairly. If a great number of bids have been received it may be necessary to arrive at a shortlist. It will usually be immediately apparent that some bids will not fulfil the product specification or other aspects of the invitation to tender – the prospective supplier may be considered too small to cope with the requirements or may not be financially stable, for example, and these can be ruled out.

Next it will be necessary to evaluate the bids. This should include:

- Checking the supplier's credentials – do they have the experience and capacity to supply?
- Matching the offer to the product specification – does what is offered fulfil all the requirements for the product or service to be supplied?
- Seeking clarification where necessary.
- Evaluating the mix of cost, quality, delivery requirements and reliability that is offered to arrive at the best match.

Evaluating a bid can be a complicated process and it helps if the selection criteria are laid out in advance and the different aspects prioritised. It is imperative that there is complete fairness in both the tendering and evaluation processes.

The final step in the tendering process is to offer a contract to the successful bidder and advise all other bidders of the outcome. At this point you should be ready to answer any queries that may arise from this. Many prospective suppliers will expect and welcome feedback on the process.

SUMMARY

In this chapter we looked at the subject of suppliers. Selecting the right supplier to suit the organisation must take into account the organisation's requirements, the quality and suitability of what is offered, the price, aspects of the service such as prompt deliveries, and the reputation of prospective suppliers.

Next we discussed ways to find suppliers including by recommendation, from directories or the press, at exhibitions and conferences or via Chambers of Commerce.

(Continued)

(Continued)

The first step to appointing the right supplier is to clarify what is required. Next it will be necessary to negotiate with suppliers and, apart from the obvious aspect of price, there are several other aspects to consider such as delivery, payment terms, the product and the supplier's reputation and service.

Having chosen a supplier it is then necessary to build a good working relationship. This requires understanding on both sides plus, usually, formalised agreements and regular performance reviews.

Finally, we looked at the formal tendering process that is often used for larger supply contracts and the procedures that must be followed.

ACTION CHECKLIST

1. Consider the suppliers used by your organisation. How were these found?
2. What would you say is the most important thing to consider when looking for a new supplier?
3. Does your organisation usually look for low prices when negotiating with suppliers or are there other aspects that may be more important?
4. Taking one of your organisation's suppliers as an example, think about the working relationship that has been established. Does it suit both parties?
5. Has your organisation been involved in a tendering process and, if so, what was it for and what was the outcome?

11

When should you outsource parts of the business?

Outsourcing can be a way to ensure that the organisation is able to concentrate on what it does best – its core activities – and leave other aspects of the business to those who are experts in that area. Contracting out a business function to someone else has various advantages:

- Cost savings – paying a third party to take over responsibility means that the costs for that function are fixed for a period of time. Savings in terms of staff dedicated to that function, plus the space taken up and management's time, should ensure that it is a move that increases profits.
- It leaves the organisation's management free to concentrate on, and develop, the core competencies.
- The organisation can become more responsive both to problems in the business and also to new ideas, as management will not be spending as much time sorting out the non-core competencies.

- Expertise from outside the organisation will be used. If staff already employed do not have that level of expertise this is of benefit to the company.

Although outsourcing non-core activities will produce many benefits, including those discussed above, it should not be seen as a magical solution to problems with those activities or as something that will remove all responsibility for making those activities work. Even when an outside company is providing a service that was previously done in-house, it will still be necessary to keep a check on that service. As with everything, there will be disadvantages and drawbacks. Consider the following:

- The outsourcing contract will need to be managed – it will be necessary to hold regular reviews of the contract relating to the outsourced activity. This should ensure that you are getting what was promised and that it is still relevant and working well for the organisation.
- Not all costs associated with providing the service in-house will disappear – some costs will be fixed. So, for example, the space that the activity takes up when done in-house will still be there, even when the work does not need to be done.
- There will be staff issues to deal with. This may involve redundancies or work role changes that will need to be sorted out in terms of human resources activities, retraining and so on.
- There will inevitably be some loss of control of the outsourced activity. Although the service levels and so on will be agreed in the contract, it will not be the organisation's employees doing the work – they will work for someone else.

So, the answer to the question of 'When should you outsource parts of the business?' is 'when someone else can do it better and cheaper'. Outsourcing should be considered for all aspects of an organisation's operations but it is first necessary to determine which are the core competencies. The next section will focus on identifying these.

What are your organisation's core competencies?

The first thing to do when assessing an organisation's options for outsourcing part of its business is to decide which parts should NOT be outsourced. These are the things that are at the heart of the business – they are the core competencies. So, for example, an organisation set up to manufacture machine components should not be outsourcing this manufacture unless they are having problems making them to a competitive price and quality, in which case the whole business will need to be reassessed. They could, instead, choose to outsource their payroll operation, their transport requirements or selling the product (unless they are particularly good at these aspects of the business).

So, how do you decide on the core competencies? If the activity in question plays an important role in the business strategy then it is probably a core competency. What is the business there for? What are its objectives? If, for example, the answer is 'to provide IT services to other companies', then IT is the core competency and obviously cannot be outsourced. But if the answer is 'to provide machine parts' and IT is used to produce invoices and so on within the organisation, then manufacture is the core competency and it will usually be possible to outsource the IT function.

However, just because an activity is not a core competency does not mean that it should automatically be outsourced. If the appropriate level of expertise exists within the organisation to provide the service in question, it will be necessary to think long and hard about outsourcing. Activities are usually contracted out to specialist providers of those services.

Let's look at some of the areas of a business that are commonly outsourced.

Information technology provision

This function includes managing internal systems and software, and managing the network used in the organisation. It may also include building and maintaining the organisation's website.

Cleaning and catering

These are usually non-core competencies that can cause problems if provided in-house, so will be outsourced as a matter of routine in many organisations.

Human resources (HR)

All or part of the HR function in an organisation can be contracted out – either on a full-time or an 'as and when' basis. This could include employee relations management, dispute management, recruitment, personnel record keeping and so on.

Health and safety

Where there is a need for legal compliance, as in the case of health and safety, it is often necessary to outsource the function to take advantage of specialist knowledge.

Marketing

Marketing activities such as advertising, public relations, customer surveys and customer communications can be outsourced with great success. It may also be possible to outsource the sales function to an agency that specialises in the type of product or service produced by the organisation.

Accounting functions

It is possible to outsource the whole accounting process – invoicing, tax statements, payroll, producing final accounts and auditing. These are almost always non-core competencies so are commonly outsourced with great success. Not only can costs be reduced in this way but there is also greater security in letting experts handle financial matters like these.

Transport

Deliveries can be undertaken at lower cost by specialist transport companies and this will mean that the outsourcing business does not have to run and maintain a fleet of vehicles. The administration function associated with deliveries is also routinely outsourced.

Customer care

Some of the activities associated with customer care can be outsourced. This may include carrying out surveys to gauge reaction to new products and responding to customer queries, order taking and so on. There are specialist agencies that run call centres to deal with customer care issues such as these.

Many of these activities can be outsourced with confidence as they will bring valuable expertise to the function which, if being dealt with in-house, would not have been available. Higher standards can therefore often be achieved.

Making a case for outsourcing

Having decided upon the activity to be considered for outsourcing, the pros and cons can be listed to make a business case for (or against) taking this action. The main criteria for deciding whether or not to outsource an activity are outlined below.

Cost

If it is possible to get the same (or better) results from outside the organisation at a cost that is less than the total cost to the organisation of providing the service for itself then that activity is an ideal candidate for outsourcing. In addition to the amount that the supplier of the activity will charge there will be other costs to take into account. It is important not to ignore the costs that will remain with the organisation. These costs could include:

● Managing the relationship with the supplier – although the actual activity will not have to be carried out in-house, it will be necessary to maintain some level of control within the organisation. Someone will have to be given the responsibility for ensuring that the service is being provided to the agreed standards and for resolving possible problems and disagreements between the two organisations.

- Existing staff costs – this could include redundancy payments or reorganisation and retraining costs for members of staff whose jobs are affected by the decision to outsource.
- Space – unless one of the reasons for outsourcing the function was a lack of space to carry it out in-house, it is likely that the space previously occupied will either be left empty or occupied by another, expanding department. Either way, that space will incur costs such as heating, lighting, business rates, rent (or a proportion of mortgage or loan costs), fulfilling health and safety requirements and so on.

A careful check of all these costs will soon show whether or not a decision to outsource would be a wise one.

Expertise

If sufficient expertise, experience and staff resources do not exist within the organisation to carry out the function to an acceptable level then there are only two choices – to buy in the resources or to outsource the function. Before making a final decision to outsource on this basis, a thorough review of the alternatives in this respect should be carried out.

- Are there members of staff who could be trained to provide the required service? It's often a good idea to check with staff to confirm their previous experience – there may already be the required expertise in-house that has not been discovered.
- Could existing departments be reorganised? For instance, a customer care function could be split into smaller sections relating to specific product areas that

could be absorbed by production or marketing
departments.
● Is there spare capacity in other departments? It may be
possible to allocate the work done within the department
whose function is under review to other departments. For
example, invoicing can often be done at the point of
dispatch rather than requiring a specialised department.
● Could the function in question be provided in-house in a
different form? For example, in the case of a catering
function that is under review, it may be possible to
replace a fully staffed canteen with a more limited service
to include vending machines or a more basic menu.

All of these factors regarding expertise must be taken into account
and carefully costed so that a case can be made for – or against –
outsourcing.

Although cost and the availability of expertise are the main
issues when considering outsourcing, many other factors are often
allowed to come into play and some of these are covered below.

Sentiment

People do like to stick with what they know and may be reluctant
to let a 'treasured' function go. There may be loyalties within an
organisation that can cloud the judgement of even the best
managers. It can seem to be an impossible notion to get rid of
something that people enjoy or are proud of and this will mean that
the case in favour of outsourcing is never adequately considered
or even, in extreme cases, may not even be brought up.
Sometimes it is necessary to mount a campaign of communication
to convince people that this is merely sentiment and does not
make an effective business case for keeping the function.

History

Just because 'this is the way that it has always been done' it does not mean that changes cannot be beneficial to an organisation. There will always be resistance to change but a case must be made if it is decided that outsourcing is the best option in the current circumstances. Again, extensive communication may be necessary to convince people who are resistant to change.

Power struggles

Sometimes people can feel under threat when change is proposed and will see the change as an attempt to remove power and control from them or to favour one manager or department over another. Many actions that are counter-productive may be taken in an effort to hold on to power or to come out on top when the decision creates competition for resources between managers and departments.

Lack of knowledge

Not knowing what is available outside the organisation can mean that all the possible solutions to a problem – including outsourcing – are not considered. It is the responsibility of senior managers in any organisation to inform themselves as to what their competitors are doing – are they outsourcing certain aspects of the business? Are they cutting back on non-core functions? They should also be fully aware of what is available. They can keep informed on matters like these in a number of ways including reading trade magazines, networking and keeping in touch with trade bodies, Chambers of Commerce and so on.

Having conducted this thorough examination and decided that outsourcing will be the best option, a case must then be made. It may be that this case is to be submitted for approval (or information) to a number people, for example:

- Stakeholders such as senior management and shareholders – they may need to be convinced of the viability of any plan to outsource major parts of a business. This will include the financial implications of the move and it will be necessary to be specific about the cost of the service to be provided and of any extra costs – as detailed above – that will be incurred.
- Members of staff whose jobs are to be replaced by the outsourcing (and their representatives) may need to be negotiated with and to be convinced of the need to make the savings where applicable. Communication about the reasons for the changes is very important in this case.
- Members of staff who are staying in their existing departments – they will be worried that their jobs are under threat so, again, communication will play an important part in minimising disruption.
- Customers – it is vital that customers are informed in the right way of any changes that may affect them. It is always a good idea to inform customers before they get to hear from other, less positive sources such as competitors or disgruntled employees. If any change can be presented in a positive light and the advantages pointed out then it will always be more readily accepted and will have less impact on the business.
- Existing suppliers – here again, reassurance may be necessary to ensure continued supplies if the situation is seen as threatening.

Whoever the case for outsourcing is to be considered by, it should address the following issues.

Cost

This will be the main driving factor in most cases where outsourcing is recommended and some stakeholders (directors, banks, etc.) will be particularly swayed by a case that predicts appreciable cost savings. The case for outsourcing should be particularly specific in this area – it should not be taken for granted that outsourcing automatically results in cost savings. It may be, of course, that a better service will be provided at the same, or greater, cost.

Effect on other parts of the business

In making a case for outsourcing, other benefits, apart from cost savings, must be examined and, where applicable, emphasised. It may be that the employees who have previously been supplying the service to be outsourced are freed to concentrate on other areas of the business. This will have a positive effect on the business. For example, where IT functions are outsourced, it may be that relatively inexperienced members of staff have been spending too much time on – and also getting frustrated by – small problems with software and having someone to sort out these problems for them will not only free up time but will also result in quicker production of invoices or schedules, order entry and so on.

Improvements

Can the organisation offer an improved service or product as a result of outsourcing the function? If so, the case must include details of the improvements, what the effect on the profitability of the organisation will be and who will be affected in terms of customers and also freeing up management time to concentrate on other issues within the business. These improvements may come as a direct result of the new service which could utilise greater expertise or resources, or less directly in terms of allowing other areas of the business to be managed more effectively.

Competitive advantage

As a result of outsourcing many companies find that they can gain a competitive advantage in the market in which they are operating. The many benefits of outsourcing – greater control of costs, the releasing of capital employed in the business and the increased flexibility – can prove to be an advantage in a competitive market. One example of a competitive advantage that may be gained by outsourcing is where IT provision is outsourced. This may result in the latest technology being used, meaning that work can be more efficient, giving customers and suppliers quicker responses and so on.

Expertise

One undoubted advantage that many organisations are able to show when outsourcing is that they gain access to greater expertise than they previously had when the function was provided in-house. By selecting a supplier that specialises in the service to be outsourced it is possible to utilise this greater skill without having to employ the often expensive experts full time.

Whatever the focus of the case being made for outsourcing, it should be presented in a clear way, with all benefits quantified and summarised. It should be aimed at the people who are to make the decision and take into account their particular interests. So, for example, if the main decision will be made by financial people then the cost savings could be emphasised by going into a high level of detail about where the savings will be made while reassuring about the service levels, but if the decision about this is to be made by a sales or marketing director in respect of a product to be manufactured outside the company, then the benefits of the new product will need to be brought to the fore.

INSTANT TIP

As soon as the decision has been made to outsource a function a way of communicating with all concerned should be set up to lessen the negative impact of any changes.

Assessing the impact on staff

Outsourcing can have an effect on people employed in the area to be outsourced long before the change is made. From the point when the idea of outsourcing is first considered by senior management there will be rumours and concern among the people who may be affected. Although confidentiality is important it can be almost impossible to stop speculation even at this very early stage in the development of a policy on outsourcing so there will inevitably be an impact on staff.

Following the early planning stages when the idea of outsourcing may first be considered, there will be a phase of information gathering. At this point, most of the staff involved will have to be consulted or, at the least, their jobs examined. This is important to establish that the function as it operates in-house can at least be equalled. Incoming suppliers may wish to employ some

– or all – of the staff currently employed in providing the function so they will need details of what is being done and by whom. This only serves to heighten the effect on staff working in that area.

So, it can be seen that there will be an impact on employees in the department concerned and this, in turn, can affect the morale and motivation of staff throughout the organisation. This can range from a slight unease to severe anxiety that may result in stress and increased sickness absence.

It is important to begin a campaign of communication with affected departments at the very early stages to minimise this impact. People will be concerned that their jobs will disappear or, at the very least, will change considerably. This communication should have two purposes:

1. To inform and reassure employees.
2. To gauge the effect of the changes on staff.

The first of these two reasons for communicating at a time of major change in an organisation, to inform and reassure employees, will be necessary to mitigate the effect that a pending decision to outsource will have. This includes the effect on the employees and the effect on the business. Employees may suffer from stress which, as mentioned earlier, can lead to absenteeism, with its obvious effect, in turn, on the business. Even if the stress and unease that arises is not serious enough to cause sickness there may well be a reduction in efficiency and effectiveness in the department concerned. Any meaningful and carefully considered communication that can be imparted to employees will lessen this effect. The methods of communication that will prove successful will vary according to the organisation, the numbers of people involved, their locations and the size of the changes to be made. These methods could include some or all of the following:

● company-wide intranet
● newsletters

- notice boards
- team, departmental or one-to-one meetings.

Assessing the reaction of staff to changes is important so that changes can be handled in the most appropriate way. Methods of communication that will assist with this task include:

- team meetings with opportunity for feedback during the meeting
- staff surveys – these should usually be confidential
- announcements calling for staff comments
- consultation meetings held with staff representatives.

The most important point to note in assessing the impact on staff is that it should be done from the very early stages in order to avoid an escalation of the effects of the changes on staff.

Where the act of outsourcing means that reductions in staff numbers (or getting rid of an entire department) are inevitable then three options must be considered:

1. Transfer of employment – in many cases where a business takes over a function from another there will be a transfer of many staff from one company to another to carry on providing the service. This provides continuity and makes the best use of the skills and experience available. These staff will usually then have their terms and conditions of employment changed to those applied by their new employers but agreements are often made that will lead to further changes. This may include travelling allowances and maintaining pay scales for a set period of time. Often only a proportion of the employees will be needed as the new company may bring in their own managers and so on and others will be surplus to requirements. The employees who will have to leave will need to be given one of the other two options.

2. Redeployment – this option, where staff are given alternative work roles in another area of the business, is preferable to redundancy in that it is better for staff morale, saves costs and keeps valuable skills within the business. In large organisations when this is not possible immediately, employees whose jobs will not exist following outsourcing are usually put on a redeployment register and the human resources department will offer a range of help. This can include assessment for other duties, additional training, and assistance with locating another position within the organisation. They may also help with looking for a job outside the organisation, writing CVs, etc.

3. Redundancy – this is often an expensive option but may be the only way to resolve the issue. There are statutory requirements for the amount of notice that must be given, how this notice must be given and the payments that must be made according to the age of the employee and their length of service. If there is a requirement to make more than twenty employees redundant the Department of Business, Innovation & Skills must be informed in writing and the employees' workplace representatives must be consulted. It is vital that an organisation in a redundancy situation is aware of, and follows, the correct procedures to avoid expensive and time-consuming problems later.

Employers have a duty of care to employees so it is always wise to ensure that staff are kept informed to avoid the unnecessary stress that can arise in times of uncertainty. The results of not considering the impact on staff and communicating with them fully during the period of change created by outsourcing can be extremely detrimental to any organisation. These include severe disruption, legal problems, absenteeism, a falling off of performance throughout the business and unnecessary levels of stress for all concerned.

Careful examination of the effect on staff is therefore necessary and the appropriate actions taken to mitigate these effects.

Selecting suppliers

There are a number of very important factors that must be considered when selecting suppliers to ensure that a long-term, effective partnership is possible. This selection process will require a detailed examination of potential suppliers.

Reputation

This is a matter of examining the supplier organisation's track record carefully. It will be necessary to ascertain how it has performed in relation to service and customer satisfaction. Are they recognised as a reputable supplier within your industry or their own?

The product or service

This is central to the agreement, of course. It must be right for the buying organisation in terms of quality and quantity, supplied at the right price and provided when and where required. If all these criteria cannot be satisfied by a potential supplier then it is unlikely to be the right one with which to enter into a long-term contract.

Finances

If a large contract is to be agreed that may entail a long-term commitment on both sides then it is essential that the supplier organisation is financially sound. This can be ascertained using copies of the company's accounts, running a credit check on them and obtaining a reference from their bank.

Getting the information on these factors to enable a decision to be made will require a lot of work. It may entail:

- Internet research – the potential service provider's website will usually provide a lot of information such as how long established, who their customers are, details about their service or product, awards they may have won, information about senior management, a mission statement and financial information. Other internet resources such as Companies House will provide other vital pieces of information.
- Paper-based research – if all the necessary details are not available on the internet, then it may be necessary to get information from organisations such as Chambers of Commerce, Trade Associations, Business Link and so on as well as obtaining copies of marketing material from the potential supplier.
- Visiting potential suppliers – when a shortlist has been drawn up of potential suppliers it will be necessary to pay a visit to each one to form impressions of the viability of the supplier organisation and to see if the two organisations will be able to work successfully together. Such visits will present an opportunity to find out about how they manage, what IT systems they use, the number of staff they will have available to service a contract with you and so on.
- Obtaining references – what experiences have others had with the potential supplier? Who are their customers? Are their relationships with existing customers long-lasting? How do they resolve disputes and complaints? To find this sort of information it will be necessary to approach organisations – preferably of a similar size and perhaps in the same industry.

Agreeing a contract for an outsourced service

A contract must set out details of all aspects of the service to be provided and will involve the obligations and requirements of both the supplier and the buyer and specify the standards to be achieved. Compensation is usually also specified in the event that the service levels are not achieved. The following must be included:

- A comprehensive description of the service to be provided.
- Price and payment terms.
- Service levels – when will the service be provided, how often, quality, management arrangements, reports to be provided and so on.
- Responsibilities of both the supplier and the buyer.
- Penalty clauses to be paid in the event of service failure.
- Legal requirements.
- A system of performance review and monitoring.
- How changes to the service level agreement can be made and in what circumstances. In the life of a long contract markets and requirements will change so the agreement must allow for this.
- The procedures to be followed in the event of a dispute.
- How the contract can be terminated.
- Renewal date when the contract comes to an end or can be renegotiated.

These service level agreements are the subject of much discussion and negotiation and will require legal input to ensure that what is agreed is exactly what was intended and that both parties to the agreement are protected. Outsourcing contracts are usually long-term arrangements that involve a large commitment on both sides so it is essential that everyone is happy with the arrangements and views them as being for the benefit of everyone.

Outsourcing contracts can involve putting in place staff and assets and it can therefore be difficult to bring the function back in-house when the contract comes to an end. There may be assets such as IT equipment and software, for example, that will need to be removed from the customer's premises or staff who will have to leave the contract at its end. For this reason, it is useful to give some consideration to what will happen at the end of the contract. Of course, it is preferable to renew the contract but this does not always happen and the consequences of not having made any preparation for this can be disastrous for a business. A strategy for dealing with the end of a contract – however it ends – should be clear and comprehensive.

Monitoring performance against the contract

In any service level agreement a system of monitoring performance should be specified. There will be standards set that can be measured periodically throughout the life of the contract. These standards will differ according to the function being outsourced and the industry in which the organisation operates but will usually cover:

- Costs – a careful and constant check will have to be made to ensure the expected cost is what is actually being paid.
- Customer reaction – if the service has any impact on customers of the organisation (and most things that happen within an organisation have the potential to affect customers) their reaction should be monitored. This might be done via a formal customer survey or, more informally, by staff who have customer contact reporting comments received and so on. Sales figures should also be

monitored as customers may decrease their orders – or not order at all – if they feel that service levels have been adversely affected.

- Lead times – outsourcing contracts can often be entered into in an effort to reduce lead times. Even if this is not a central issue, the effect of outsourcing on lead times, i.e. the time between receipt of order and delivery, should be carefully monitored.
- On-time deliveries – the percentage of deliveries that arrive on time should be monitored as this is an important part of customer service and a poor delivery record will quickly impact on sales.
- Product defects – again, a check on this will control adverse effects.
- Complaints – if any complaint is received in any organisation at any time it should be recorded but this is especially important during times of great change such as when a function is outsourced. The complaints should then be analysed to find out where – and why – problems are occurring.
- Returns – if applicable, the amount of product being returned must be recorded as a measure of customer satisfaction. As in the case of complaints, the reasons for return should be recorded and analysed.

Some or all of the above should be monitored and the results acted upon. Producing records and complicated reports can be very satisfying but what is really important is taking action according to what is found from an analysis of the figures and reports. So, for example, in the case of an outsourced invoicing function if mistakes are reported the reason for the mistakes must be found and corrected as soon as possible. Mistakes in invoices will quickly lead to a cash flow problem when customers refuse to pay incorrect invoices. Any delay in sorting out the problem will impact severely on cash flow.

It is a relatively simple task to compare results from before and after the implementation of any new system. When reports are produced the person responsible for monitoring and managing the outsourcing contract should be able to spot trends that show whether or not a problem is just a 'blip' or is an increasing problem that requires urgent action.

In addition to ongoing monitoring of reports on the service level standards, it will be necessary to conduct regular reviews to make sure that everything is going to plan and that the benefits that were anticipated are being realised. Monitoring standards is not a one-off job. The schedule for reviews should be set when the contract is being negotiated.

The service level agreement will, in effect, have identified a number of Key Performance Indicators (KPIs) that, when measured, will indicate whether or not targets are being met. KPIs should be quantifiable and measured as part of normal work processes and will be closely linked to the organisation's objectives. There are management information systems software products available that will do this measuring on a regular basis.

Of course, there may be areas where performance is important to the organisation but that are not easy to measure in a quantitative way in order to produce KPIs. Where qualitative information is produced it must be treated with caution. However, such information can be very useful in helping to see just what is going on and evaluating the success of the outsourcing.

At this point, when the reviews are undertaken, it is a good time to recognise achievement and hard work by the people involved and ensure that all employees of both organisations are made aware of the gains, benefits and improvements that have been made as a result of outsourcing.

INSTANT TIP

One last point about outsourcing – is it possible to gain any positive publicity from it? Putting a positive spin on a major change within an organisation, such as outsourcing a function, is sometimes a good idea. If, for example, the IT function is to be outsourced, a press release to local newspapers and the trade press announcing the improvements that are expected as a result may well produce a good news story.

SUMMARY

This chapter examined the subject of outsourcing. This is where an organisation concentrates on its core activities and contracts out other business functions to another organisation. This is usually in order to make cost savings and to leave management free to develop the activities at which the organisation excels.

We looked at how to decide which activities to outsource. Apart from core activities, this could include almost anything that someone else can do better and/or cheaper. Many activities are commonly outsourced including IT provision, cleaning, catering, human resources management, marketing, health and safety management, transport, customer care and accounting functions.

It is usually necessary to make a business case for outsourcing focusing on the cost savings and expertise that may be offered by the supplier and on the competitive advantage that may be gained. We also looked at what may prevent outsourcing in organisations. Quite often

(Continued)

(Continued)

organisations are resistant to change and this may mean that outsourcing is not considered. Other barriers may include power struggles within the organisation and not knowing what is available outside the organisation.

We saw that existing staff can be severely affected by outsourcing a function and that clear and comprehensive communication is especially important at this time. We also considered the three options for dealing with the employment of the affected employees – transfer of employment to the supplier, redeployment within the organisation and redundancy.

We then went on to how to select the right outsourcing partner and then agree a contract where all relevant aspects of the service to be provided are detailed. This often takes the form of a service level agreement with agreed penalties in the event of service failure. As always, performance must be monitored and we looked at ways to do this.

ACTION CHECKLIST

1. Does your organisation outsource any functions? If so, what are they?
2. Are there other functions that, in your opinion, could be outsourced?
3. What is your organisation's core activity?
4. Have you any experience of when a function has been outsourced? If so, what happened to the employees involved?
5. Do you have access to a service level agreement? If not, could you plan one out for a function within your department?

12

The Companion Interview: Dianne Thompson on managing activities and resources

The following interview with Dianne Thompson CBE was conducted by Ed Peppitt, author of *Six of the Best* (Hodder 2007). It was updated in late 2010 in conjunction with Hodder to reflect changes to the business since then, including Camelot winning the third Licence to operate the UK National Lottery in 2008 and the sale of shares in the business to the Ontario Teachers' Pension Plan in 2010.

Dianne joined Camelot in February 1997 as their first female Executive Director and was appointed Chief Executive after Camelot was awarded the second National Lottery Licence in December 2000.

As Group CEO of Camelot, Dianne has since then developed and driven a strategy for growth which in 2009/10 delivered the second best ever total sales and the highest returns to Good Causes in a decade. Camelot raises more than £25 million a week for good causes and has created over 2,500 millionaires to date.

Dianne consistently features in the top 10 of Marketing magazine's Power 100 list of UK marketing community's most influential players and in September 2006 she was awarded the Chartered Management Institute's Gold Medal for her strategic direction and leadership.

Dianne was named Veuve Clicquot Business Woman of the Year in 2000 and was awarded a CBE in the 2006 New Year's honours list for services to Business.

Ed Peppitt writes:

In today's high-pressured, time-poor environments, how can leaders and managers ensure that their staff are effective and motivated in their daily work? Is the drive for efficiency the responsibility of the individual or the organisation as a whole? How does the culture of the organisation affect its operational management? To have most impact, should a leader focus most attention on managing teams, or are energies better spent on optimising financial resources?

These were just a few of the challenges that I wanted to discuss with Dianne Thompson, as I arrived at Camelot's London office. Dianne was busy on the telephone as I took my seat, immediately reinforcing my assumption that she worked a relentless schedule. This seemed a good place to start to find out how Dianne regards all the various competing demands on her time.

Pressure and the work/life balance

Behind the principle of needing to manage activities and resources effectively, there is this assumption that today's workplace is 'high-pressured' and 'time-poor'.

High-pressured, time-poor – is that how you see your working life?

It is certainly how I see my working life, but I try very hard for that not to be the case for the rest of my people. I always describe Camelot as a way of life and not a job, but I do try very hard to make sure that the rest of the team get some sense of normality. To make sure that this is re-enforced throughout the company, we have a number of policies which have been devised to make sure that staff are protected and that they are able to maintain a healthy work/life balance while carrying out their often demanding jobs.

For example, we have comprehensive arrangements in place to allow flexible working practices like job sharing, phased return to work after prolonged leave, working from home and extended maternity benefits.

We do also have a comprehensive reward structure in place at Camelot to maintain the high performance culture that we have worked hard to put in place. We have annual progression pay reviews, an annual bonus scheme, an instant reward scheme, as well as private health insurance, subsidised health club membership, company phones and cars, and a pension scheme where Camelot matches employee contributions by up to 7.5 per cent.

You said Camelot is a way of life, not just a job. What does that mean?

Well, we have daily draws now, we have three big draw nights a week – on a Wednesday, Friday and Saturday. So there are big retail peaks, and that makes us as close to being a retailer as you can get without actually being one. So when I get home at night, I look at the daily sales that have been sent to me. We are also more or less always a 24-hour business as people can play interactively now – through mobile phones and on the internet – so even when the shops are closed the business doesn't stop. Senior managers within the business take turns at being the duty manager so there is someone on call all the time – and I do my share of these stints, sometimes having to take calls through the night if big projects are happening and decisions need to be made there and then. So the job is there, all the time.

We are unique in that we are a private company but in a public goldfish bowl, and everything we do is under the utmost scrutiny, which is how it should be. But as the head of the company I need to be available nearly all the time.

So is there a 'typical working day' for you?

No, probably not, but I am not complaining. I absolutely love what I do. I try to have a bit of normality around the week. I try very hard to be in Watford (our head office) on Mondays and Fridays. I listen to feedback, and I'm often hearing people say that they 'like to see Di around'. So at least everybody in Watford knows that unless something unusual happens, I'll be there all day Monday and all day Friday. From Tuesday to Thursday, because of the nature of what we do, I tend to be in London, because that's where the media and the government are. In a typical week I try to limit the number of dinners I attend to two.

You do have to achieve the balance, because as I have said, Camelot is a way of life and not a job.

I have a quote here from Sir Martin Sorrell saying that women are much better than men at handling the work/life balance. I also have a quote from you saying: 'I'm just a workaholic. It is difficult to get

the balance right!' Is that still the case? Are you a workaholic?

I *am* a workaholic, but I think that is because of my background. I am the product of a Northern working-class family. My parents chose to have just one child to be able to give that child the opportunities they didn't have themselves. My dad, who is incredibly bright, had a place to go to grammar school but couldn't because his family needed him to go to work. It was a different generation. So they took the decision that they desperately wanted a family, but that they would only have one child so they could give that child the benefits that they hadn't had. And that child was me. So I think that they bred in me this sort of work ethic. That is where the drive came from, I think.

I became driven because I was trying to prove to them that their sacrifice was worthwhile. It is certainly where the inspiration came from. And, you know, people ask me if I have had mentors or role models. Well, my role models were my parents, because they tried so very hard. They brought me up to realise that you don't get anything for nothing, and that if you want something in life you have got to work for it.

I remember reading that while you were lecturing full-time at Manchester Polytechnic, you were also setting up and running your own advertising agency. Is that what you mean by working hard?

I like a challenge! The job at the Polytechnic was a sort of accident. I had worked for six years at ICI and it became clear to me that it was time for a change. I was invited to join ICI's fast track programme, which would have led me to a career in organics or petrochemicals. Flattered as I was, I knew that it wasn't for me. It made me think more carefully about my next step though and I realised that I wanted to 'give something back'. It might sound a little arrogant now – but that's what I wanted to do at the time.

Why do you think that was arrogant?

I think it was because I felt I had nothing to learn. The college persuaded me that they wanted people from industry to come in and give the students the benefit of some real experience. So I really did think I was going there to 'give', but that it would also be a very good time for me to think about what I wanted to do next. In reality, I learned so much and actually stayed there for seven years. Again, I was very lucky, because it gave me the opportunity to start my own advertising agency. It worked perfectly because the college was desperate to have people who were real, active practitioners, so they were keen to support me in starting the agency. And we were able to employ placement students in the agency while also getting agency clients to come into the college and do guest lectures as well.

People and the importance of culture

You only have to spend five minutes with Dianne Thompson to realise that she regards the people around her as her greatest resource. From the way I was welcomed at Camelot's reception desk, and then greeted by Dianne's colleague Charlotte, it was obvious that Camelot employees are a happy breed. I had read a number of articles and interviews with Dianne, where she had reinforced, time and again, just how vital the people at Camelot are to the company's success. I wanted to find out more.

One quotation stayed with me. About her staff, Dianne said, 'I know them and they know me'. Not unusual, one might think, until you realise that Camelot employs 760 people. I needed to find out the skills a manager needs to instil that degree of familiarity with almost 800 people.

How do you foster familiarity with a thousand people?

Well you see I am very lucky because we are a huge company. Our turnover last year was more than £5 billion. But we employ fewer than 800 people. In fact, it is currently about 760. We are an SME (small and medium sized enterprise), and in an average year I get to see everybody at least twice. I try to get around all our sites. We have a warehouse in Northampton and sites in London and Aintree and our biggest site at Watford, which is the head office.

As well as it being a conscious effort on my part to have that personal contact with as many of the staff as I can, there is also a lot of media interest in Camelot which allows the staff to find out more about me than they may do in less public facing companies. People will always stop me on the stairs and ask about how my daughter is getting on, how her degree was going, how her job is going – and this is from information they've read in an interview that has appeared that week. And I think that's great – it creates a good working atmosphere.

So you don't mind that level of familiarity with your staff?

No, not at all. In fact I encourage it. We have worked very hard since 2001 to change the culture at Camelot after the company emerged battle-scarred and weary after the second lottery licence bid in 2000. You may remember that we had a long, drawn-out legal battle before we finally won the second licence. And that had taken its toll on the staff. By May 2001 we had lost one-third of the staff because while I had been out there fighting to try to save the business, everybody else was out there looking for another job. And who could blame them? We all have mortgages or rent and everything else to pay for.

By May 2001 I had a company of 500 staff, trying to do the work of 800. And, all the time, we were trying to recruit and induct and train new people. So it was vital that we initiated a massive culture change to revitalise the company and to drive it forward. We really needed to change the culture almost overnight if we were going to succeed.

We started by taking the senior managers, of which at that time there were probably about 80, away in groups of about twenty on a three-day cultural programme called 'Winning Ways'. We all had some ideas of the values in the company, and we went away to question whether these values were still valid in the new world we are in. If they were valid, how do we make sure that we get them embedded in the company, and do we need to have a set of behaviours that actually typify what we expect the values to be?

We had the mnemonic 'FITTER'. It stands for:

We believe in **F**air play

We believe in total **I**ntegrity (We are totally honest, totally transparent. We have to be that way, because if ever you had any doubt about the integrity of the Lottery, then the Lottery is dead.)

We believe in **T**eam work

We are **T**rusted to deliver

We strive for **E**xcellence

We are **R**esponsible to all our stakeholders (Camelot is unusual because we have a massive number of stakeholders; from 30 to 40 million players a week, to retailers operating over 28,500 lottery terminals, to government, our regulator, 14 lottery distributors, public interest groups and NGOs – the list goes on.)

So those were our values beforehand. Then we went away and asked ourselves whether they were still valid for us today. And we agreed that, yes, they were. So how do we embed them in the company and what behaviour do we want to see?

I think that we demonstrate a number of behaviours, including creativity and a partnering attitude, but another very important behaviour that we believe in is *passion*. I know that you could talk to virtually anybody who works for Camelot, and they would agree. We are just passionate about what we do. We get up each morning to go to work to make Britain a better place. That's what we do!

But you are clearly proud of it?

I'm desperately proud of it. Camelot has helped to raise over £25 billion for good causes, which has helped to fund over 340,000 individual awards up and down the UK. That's in addition to what's gone into the Treasury in Lottery Duty. It has transformed the face of Britain and has paid for the biggest period of civic regeneration since Victorian times. How amazing is that?! Plus, we've now created more than 2,500 lottery millionaires!

I'd really like to investigate this culture a little more deeply. I can see how at head office in Watford, you could look around you, and you'd notice straight away if someone wasn't displaying one of those values, particularly the passion value. But you've got almost 800 staff. How can you be so confident that you all share the same values? How would you know if someone wasn't demonstrating the Camelot culture?

Everybody is targeted with living the Camelot values and those values are instilled in the company all the way through. I am very privileged because I run a big company, we do a huge amount for good causes for Britain, and yet we are only 800 people, so we know each other. If you are in ICI with 200,000 people, how do you do that?

But there are companies with 40 people who don't have that, who are thinking 'how on earth do you do it with 1,000?'

The answer is, you need to be open and transparent.

It's as simple as that?

It's as simple as that. You are open and transparent, you communicate well, and you are passionate about what you do. It is a standing joke, but you can slice any one of us inside and we are like a stick of rock that says 'Camelot' or 'National Lottery' all the way through.

We are all working towards the same end.

And that's clearly something that exists informally in Camelot as well as formally? You have teams, and there are team structures, but it seems as though this team spirit comes pretty naturally?

Yes, I think it does. I think we learnt the hard way during our bid for the licence in 2000.

During a judicial review which became part of that competition, Camelot had such a high profile that the media were reporting on events incredibly quickly and before we had even had a chance to talk to the staff ourselves. So they were finding out what was going on from the television – which is not how I believe it should be!

It was a defining moment for me to understand that you can't always control your messages or the timing of when information is released. I realised then that we had to revise our mechanisms for talking to our staff quickly.

So we created our 'cascade process', and every Monday the executive team at Camelot has a meeting at ten o'clock, which lasts about an hour when we review what has happened over the last week, any issues we have, and what is going to happen that coming week. We decide on anything that the staff collectively need to know. We agree on the five or six points that should be cascaded throughout the company and then each of us cascades these key points to six or seven people. They, in turn, have a team of people to cascade to, and by 12 o'clock everybody in the company has received the key points of that week's meeting.

It keeps everybody informed, involved and very much part of the business – rather than perhaps feeling isolated in their own particular area.

What's the opposite of cascade? How would I, as a junior member of staff at Camelot, get a message back up to you?

Quite easily actually, because everybody knows that they are more than welcome to email me, or come and see me, or ring me. I have an open door policy. In a typical week, I would say that I probably get 20 or 30 emails from staff, with questions or suggestions for improvement.

But on a more formal level we also have a 'Staff Consultative Forum', which is a group elected to represent all of the departments in the company. The elections are supervised by

ACAS, so it is all externally monitored and verified. The forum meets every month as a body, and once a quarter they meet formally with me and the HR Director, so I am there by their invitation. That is their opportunity to share ideas with me, and I share my ideas with them.

They can also give me feedback on decisions we have made for the business, make suggestions for the whole business, or for their individual departments, make a complaint about something they, or members of their department are not happy with – and I take that information back to the executive team for consideration and action where necessary.

We also have a staff survey, operated and verified by an external company.

I'm intrigued by your cascading processes. I know of organisations where team leaders and managers 'filter' the information that goes back to the people at the top. In other words, they tell you what they think you want to hear. Does that exist at all here? Would you know if it did?

We don't do that at all. I think the issue is to do with integrity, as I was saying earlier. We are very fortunate that through good marketing we are here 15 years on, with 70 per cent of the adult population still playing the National Lottery. And that's because they believe it is totally fair and is run with complete integrity. The day that they don't believe that is the day that the Lottery will come to an end.

So we have to be absolutely transparent about everything that we do, and that's the way we run the business.

So if a team leader has bad news, they will come and tell you?

Yes, absolutely.

And if you had bad news, you would tell the staff?

Yes. We are all in this together and they deserve to be given the full picture, whether good or bad.

Efficiency

> 'A good manager or leader increases operational efficiency and effectiveness.'
>
> Chartered Management Institute

I wanted to talk to Dianne about business efficiency, and what it means to an organisation such as Camelot. In organisations of any size, whose responsibility is it to create efficiency? The individual employee, or the organisation as a whole? I was fortunate enough to have read before the interview that Camelot runs the most efficient lottery in Europe. I asked Dianne how lottery efficiency was measured.

It is measured by the returns to government and good causes. There's an American company called La Fleur, which analyses and reports on lotteries worldwide. They investigate how much money goes back in prizes and also how much goes to governments and good causes. Some lotteries around the world don't differentiate between government and good causes – they simply make returns to government, and then government decides on the allocation. We pay lottery duty as well as give money to good causes. So it is that percentage of the total take that goes to government which is regarded as the measure of efficiency.

Did you set out to be the most efficient lottery in Europe? Was that one of Camelot's aims from the start?

We set out to be very efficient, simply because of how the lottery pound breaks down. On average, 50 per cent of the revenue generated goes back to players in prizes; 28 per cent goes to the good causes; 12 per cent goes in lottery duty, which is obviously a statutory duty – it's not optional. So that's 90 per cent of the revenue taken care of already! Then 5 per cent goes to the retailers – they get a 5 per cent commission on every ticket that they sell. They also get a small commission for paying the low-tier prizes.

So when all of that is taken into account, I'm left with 4.8 per cent of the revenue that actually comes into Camelot. Of that 4.8 per cent I lose one percentage point immediately: because we've got lottery duty on tickets rather than VAT, I can't reclaim the VAT that we spend in the business – so my 4.8 per cent becomes 3.8 per cent. Then after all of Camelot's running costs are paid for, we are actually allowed to make half a percent profit. So it's absolutely vital that I keep the costs tightly under control – if I let them drift by only half a percent, then my shareholder wouldn't get any return at all.

No wonder you take efficiency seriously. So it is as tight as that?

It is. We are different from a lot of other lotteries. For example, many state lotteries work very differently. A typical example would be one of the European lottery's which gives back 50 per cent in prizes to the players. They will give 5 per cent, as we do, to their retailers. So that is 55 per cent allocated, and 45 per cent remains. Then they will take their costs out of that 45 per cent and whatever is left goes into government.

Because it is measured in this way, there is no real incentive for them to be very efficient at all.

In contrast, this is the only job I have ever had where I am praised for making half a percent profit – everywhere else I would have been fired!

This was extremely interesting. I realised that I had never paused to consider how the National Lottery revenue was allocated – or even the fact that Camelot does not distribute the money, but merely collects it from selling lottery tickets and then passes it straight on to the lottery distributors who then decide how it is given out. Nor how it might vary so much between lotteries around the world. Maintaining Camelot's efficiency is clearly of vital importance to Dianne Thompson. But although Dianne describes Camelot as a small organisation, it still employs almost 800 staff. How would she know if this is an efficient head count? Why not 600? What measures are in place to identify efficiencies throughout Camelot? I asked Dianne to tell me more.

We are constantly undertaking business reviews. We have a financial review group, which I chair, and we meet quarterly. But of course we have period reporting, so I am monitoring costs on a period-by-period basis.

So everything is constantly under review because, to be honest, if you are running a business on 4.8 per cent, which includes your profit, there's not much room for manoeuvre.

So would you advise any organisation to undertake the sort of efficiency reviews that Camelot does? Is the drive for efficiency as relevant to other organisations?

Well businesses usually try to be efficient because they all have shareholders. Although we are not a publicly listed company, we have a commitment, a fiduciary duty, to make profits for our shareholder. So of course there's always this pressure on us to keep our costs down and to find new ways of being more efficient.

Let me give you a very specific example of something that we have done. We had three separate call centres at one stage. We had a telesales call centre, then we had 'hotlines' as they were called, a retailer hotline and a lottery hotline, each with their own trained staff. What we have done now is to multi-skill everybody, so anybody who operates in our call centre can now do each of those three things. That in itself has allowed us to become more efficient in how many people we need answering the calls.

So where should a business start when looking to make efficiency gains?

I think all I would say is that you need to be proactive all the time. I get very frustrated with the 'if it ain't broke, don't fix it' mentality. That's not the way to run a business. The way to run a business is always to be proactive: look for efficiencies, look for ways to drive sales, to drive profits. So many people in business leave it too late, until they get into trouble. We have an annual operating plan, and we conduct quarterly reviews, so that we could see quite easily and early if we were going adrift anywhere.

Project schedules and delivery

'A good manager or leader delivers on time, to budget and to the standard required.'

Chartered Management Institute

Throughout my own career, I have worked with organisations for whom a key measure of success is the extent to which projects are delivered on time and within budget. From a personal perspective, I have lost count of the number of times I have worked late into the night, finishing a proposal or a report that had to be submitted the next day. Yet here I am interviewing the Chief Executive of Camelot, whose responsibilities include putting together bids to run the National Lottery. I remember watching on television the sealed bids to run the National Lottery being delivered to the Department of Culture, Media and the Arts back in 1994. Pallets containing boxes of paperwork were being unloaded hurriedly from lorries in an attempt to meet the midday deadline. Just what skills or efforts are required to keep a project like a lottery bid on track? What measures does Dianne Thompson have in place to ensure that the next lottery bid is delivered on time and to budget?

Right, well that's easier to answer than you might expect. I think one of the things that makes Camelot quite different from a lot of organisations is that we never get into 'steady states'. We go from one major project to another. Let me give you an example. When we won the second bid, one of the conditions of winning was that we had to install brand new terminals in every retail outlet. There was a time-frame with a financial penalty if we weren't ready on time. The penalty was £1 million a day to start with. So that focuses the mind a little bit!

So that was a massive project to get the terminals installed, and in fact we got them all in two weeks early, which was great. Then the next big challenge was to transfer all of our software systems over, which was a massive undertaking. It's similar to the process that the passport control service went through, when they got into so much trouble. So that was our next big project.

Then one of our main software suppliers got into financial difficulties in the United States and went into Chapter 11 administration. So we decided to build an ISDN network, so that we wouldn't be dependent on them. Now we own the largest private ISDN network in Europe.

Life is never straightforward at Camelot; you are literally going from one big project to the next. That's what I mean when I say that there are no 'steady states'. Everybody is working on a project at all times really.

So how would I know that the bid is on track and on budget? Well for such a big project I have a bid director, who takes responsibility for the most complicated, critical tasks. Each section of the bid has its own timeline, with a cost attributable to it for the research that might be needed to be done. There is also a separate production budget. We monitor the bid's progress at a bid steering group every week and I can see whether we are on track.

But if the pattern at Camelot is a constant flow of challenging projects, with little respite, what sort of toll does that take on you personally?

Well I am on record as saying this isn't a job, it's a way of life, and it is! It is very intrusive and very time-consuming, but I think in many ways that's part of the challenge and also part of the huge enjoyment, because you have a whole variety of different things going on all the time. It is very stimulating.

Monitoring finance

'A good manager or leader optimises use of financial and other resources.'

Chartered Management Institute

Dianne Thompson's career history comprises a number of senior marketing roles, in some of the UK's best known corporations. She has 20 years of experience working with seven-figure marketing budgets at Woolworths, ICI and Camelot. I wondered whether Dianne would have any financial advice that might apply to any organisation. After all, most of us work with marketing budgets that are a fraction of that size. So what advice would Dianne offer about marketing budgets and campaigns that might apply to smaller organisations?

Actually, I think it doesn't matter so much what the size of your budget is, because the crucial thing is the return on the investment that you are getting. At Camelot, what we have is a series of very sophisticated return-on-investment models. So everything that the marketing team does – be it a piece of television advertising or a direct mail shot or whatever – is assessed beforehand to predict what the likely return on investment will be. Then we evaluate it post-event. So over the period of 16 years that we have been running the business we have learnt very well what returns we can expect from our marketing spend.

So, for example, we know exactly what return we expect if we advertise the EuroMillions major draw that is on tonight. The EuroMillions jackpot tonight is running at about £64 million. We have been advertising very heavily during the week; I think we have done about 200 television rating points. We know exactly what sort of return we will get from that and, of course, we will evaluate it next week anyway.

But it is about making sure that you can evaluate what return you are getting so that you are using the budget that you have available in the most effective way possible.

It never occurred to me that an organisation the size of Camelot would review every flyer, every advertisement, every mailing to that extent. Do you think other organisations are complacent in that regard?

I think marketing as an industry in general is complacent, to be honest. As you probably know, I was President of the Chartered Institute of Marketing, and during my time there one of our big concerns was that too many marketers are not accountable for the money that they are spending. That is one of the reasons why boards in general find the marketing budget the easiest bit to chop because it is very difficult for some marketers to be able to defend why they need that money. By having the tools that we've got here, these return-on-investment tools, it is very easy to make a case to my board if we feel we need to spend a bit more money to do something specific.

Just to put our budget in context, it is a large budget, of course and as you would expect for a company with a turnover of more than £5 billion. It equates to about one-and-a-half per cent of our total sales revenue, but it is being spread across lots of different products. That's why we have to evaluate everything we do so thoroughly, not least because we have four of the top ten consumer brands in the UK. So the dilemma here is, for example, whether we should be giving more support to scratch cards or Thunderball? Or is the marketing budget better invested in Lotto itself? That's why we need these tools so that we can see where we get the best returns for our pound.

I know of many organisations who have separated the sales and marketing functions, and aren't able to calculate the return on investment for each marketing activity. Is that a serious mistake?

I wouldn't say it is a serious mistake, but it just means that you haven't got the information you really need to make sure you are utilising every pound of marketing spend to the very best you can.

At Camelot, we've been able to use external agencies to help us build econometric models. Take the EuroMillions Rollover today, we have got a very good idea as to whether we are likely to get better returns from television advertising or radio or printed media.

And are you saying that if an organisation like Camelot can calculate its return on investment so effectively, then organisations of any size should be able to do the same?

Yes – they may not be able to use quite the same sophisticated tools that we have, but I do think that there is a responsibility for marketers, in particular, to do their very best to evaluate the returns that they are getting for their marketing monies.

Thinking about Camelot's television advertising for a minute, how quickly would you know whether a particular campaign is achieving what you want it to achieve?

You usually know very quickly. There are two types of basic advertising that we do here. There is what we call 'generic brand advertising' and then 'specific tactical advertising', which would be for something like a Rollover or a Superdraw. With the specific tactical advertising, you know almost immediately how effective it is as it is reflected in the ticket sales.

For example, by half past seven tonight (which is the 'draw break' when tickets are no longer available to purchase for that particular draw) I will know what the sales are. I will start getting text messages on my phone from 5 p.m. today telling me what the sales are at five o'clock, at six, at seven and then at draw-break. So you know already what the impact has been.

The generic brand advertising is a little harder, but the principles are largely the same. For example, the National Lottery launched with one game in 1994 and so advertising that one brand under the crossed fingers National Lottery logo was simple and effective. However, by 2002 the lottery had expanded massively and we needed to differentiate between the different games on offer. So we launched a series of advertisements with comedian Billy Connolly, to introduce the new name for the main lottery draw as 'Lotto'.

I don't know if you remember the ads, but in one of them he was standing on a beach in Scotland and he said something like, 'Those people that run the National Lottery have decided to change its name. And guess what they are going to call it? *Lotto* ...' and then he looked incredulous at what a daft name it was. It was an educational campaign – and although it did receive some criticism within the industry, it very effectively achieved its objective with the playing public. You talk now to anybody on the street and ask them the name of the game that you play on Wednesday and Saturday, they would all say 'Lotto'. Everybody has forgotten that it used to be called the National Lottery game. So even for a generic campaign like that we had a very specific objective that needed to be met.

So you asked me how quickly we could tell if it worked. Probably on that campaign, it was about three months when you could see in our tracking research that the name change had definitely worked.

Priorities and deadlines

'A good manager or leader plans and prioritises projects and activities.'

Chartered Management Institute

One of the things that has intrigued me throughout all six interviews (for Six of the Best*) is how people like Dianne Thompson juggle competing demands on their time, and how they decide which is the priority or deadline that is most pressing. Most of us in our working lives have all or part of our agenda set for us. If you are self-employed, your priorities are set, at least in part, by your clients. If employed, then a line manager often dictates what you focus on during the working week. But what about when you are the Chief Executive of Camelot? When Dianne Thompson arrives at her desk, either in Watford or in London, how does she decide what she should devote her energies to? I needed to find out about her priorities, and what motivates her to get something done.*

That's a very good question. As I said earlier, a typical week for me would be two days at head office in Watford. I try very hard to be here on Mondays and Fridays. I like everybody here to know that they can get to see me any time, drop me an email or whatever. If I can be here more frequently then that's great, because this is head office, and this is where the bulk of my people are. But some of my job is about meeting with MPs and the media, and of course they are often based in London, so that will take me into town frequently.

I have a meeting that I chair, with my senior executives, at ten o'clock on Monday morning. For example, this coming Monday we will review what happened in the business this week. We will look at the sales for EuroMillions, we will talk about the issues that we've got coming up next week, we will be talking about the marketing activities we've planned, and those sorts of things. That will then get cascaded throughout the business, and that's how the working week starts.

On a personal level, my diary is booked up weeks and weeks in advance.

So no two weeks are the same – but there are elements that you will try to incorporate into every working week?

Yes, that's right. We have several committees, like any other organisation would. So, as I mentioned earlier, we have a Staff Consultative Forum, which is made up of representatives voted for by their colleagues, who represent the various departments in the company. They meet every month, and I meet with them once a quarter, so that's in my diary. I chair our Corporate Responsibility Board, which meets to ensure we are not only running a successful – but a responsible – National Lottery. This group meets quarterly, and that's always in my diary. We have a People Steering Group, which comprises two of my fellow Directors and me. This meets to monitor staff roles in the business, and also to consider recommendations for promotion. You asked me earlier about how I knew that 760 was an efficient head count, and whether I could be sure I had the right number of people. Well this steering group meets quarterly, and keeps that under review all the time. I also have a Finance Review Group where we make sure that our costs are on track and so on. And then there are a whole variety of other things: for example, there's an Olympic Steering Group, because as you know we have been asked to raise money for the 2012 Olympics.

So by the time you have put all of those in the diary there is a bit of a structure to my working week.

I can appreciate the variety. But given that any one of your staff would completely understand if you told them that you had been too busy to read or do something, what motivates you to get something done or finished?

Because it is a matter of personal pride, isn't it? And I am sure that that is true for most people actually. As I have said before, at Camelot we are driven by the mission that we come to work to make Britain a better place by raising as much money as we can in a socially responsible way for the good causes. When I'm out and about travelling I like to go and see projects where Lottery money is being spent. Take something like the Eden Project – it's absolutely stunning what that has done, not only for the project itself, but for Cornwall. And in London, there's Tate Modern, Tate Britain, the National Portrait Gallery, the British Museum, the Millennium Bridge, in Cardiff the Millennium Stadium, in Glasgow the Science Centre and the Falkirk Wheel a little further up in Scotland, the Odyssey in Belfast ... the list goes on. That is the pride that we all get out of what we do. That's what we do, we raise money for those projects, and that's what makes us get up and come to work, and that's what makes sure we do a damn good job and makes sure that we all meet our deadlines!

That's fantastic, but are you ever able to switch off? I have read about sportsmen and sportswomen who mentally warm up before a performance, and then unwind after it. Is that something you are able to do? Can you unwind, mentally, from one committee meeting to another?

Sometimes yes. There are times when I'll be in the car when I am heading into London from Watford. That's my thinking time. But I am very keen on getting the work/life balance right for all my people. In fact, this weekend I've got a lot of reading to do and it's not very easy to fit that into the working week. But on a typical weekend I don't work. I switch off. I will watch the lottery ticket sales with great interest on Friday night and on Saturday for the Lotto draw. I'll get the result of how many winners we've got and that is part of my weekend. But I'm very lucky. I live in a nice place, I've got a lovely garden that I'm getting back into doing. I also enjoy walking – in fact I did a 10k sponsored walk a little while ago and managed to raise £16,000 for Breast Cancer after match funding from Camelot – and the Grand Union Canal runs through the village, so there are some great canal walks. I've got lots of friends and good pubs in the village and I shall be out and about socialising. So I am very fortunate that I have a full life outside work as well, and that's what allows you to switch off. It is not about sitting down and doing nothing, it's just about getting stimulation from doing other things, I think.

But I can't claim that it has always been this way. I was always the person who worked at weekends, and when I went away on holiday I was always phoning in and checking up on people and projects. I don't do that now. I have got a very good arrangement with my PA who knows that I'm taking a week's holiday in the first week in January with my daughter. She knows exactly where I am, where I will be staying and the deal is that if she needs me, or if anybody needs me, she will be the only person who knows where I am. We also have a prearranged time of day I'll put my phone on and pick up any messages. It's not too intrusive, but it also means that I am not unreachable if I am needed. I have become very disciplined in making sure that I get the breaks at weekends and on holiday and I try very hard to ensure that my staff do the same. It would have to be a dire emergency for me to get anybody disturbed while they were on holiday.

Conclusions and recommendations

Dianne Thompson is a remarkable woman. She says that she knows her staff, and they know her. And that is absolutely true. In fact, in so many ways, she is a departure from the traditional image of a grey-suited CEO. She made me feel as welcome when interviewing her as if I had dropped by to visit a friend for a coffee. And that's the remarkable thing. I love my friends dearly, but not many of them would be able to run a global organisation with an annual turnover of more than £5 billion.

So what makes Dianne Thompson so successful? For one thing, her passion is infectious, and it is clearly what drives her. She absolutely adores what she does each day. When she says that she 'gets up each day to make Britain a better place', she means it. If you heard that from an American corporation, you would be tempted to rush to the lavatory. When Dianne Thompson says it, it seems like the most normal thing in the world. So could Dianne Thompson run the National Lottery effectively if she didn't believe wholeheartedly in what it sets out to do? I honestly don't believe that she could.

Second, she values the people around her above every other resource. It's fascinating to listen to Dianne talking, and to appreciate that she regards nearly 800 people as 'her family'. Many would argue that an organisation with a £5.4 billion turnover, and nearly 800 staff, is a large, international organisation. Yet Dianne regards Camelot as a small organisation that does a very big job. It is this that makes it clearly easier for her to create and instil the culture that so evidently exists, and which works so effectively.

Dianne admits that the essence of the National Lottery rests in its integrity: 'The day people cease to believe that the lottery is totally fair and run with complete integrity, that is the day that the Lottery will come to an end.' It's quite obvious that this integrity suits Dianne Thompson very well. She attributes much of her success with people to her open, transparent approach, and recommends this approach to any manager or leader.

This openness extends to the way that Dianne Thompson presents herself. There is no pretence, no attempt to behave or act in any way that doesn't come completely naturally. She didn't voice it, but it's absolutely clear that she has earned the respect and support of her people by being herself at all times. So do her people know Dianne as well as they think they do? The answer, I can assure you, is yes. She is a living embodiment of the phrase 'what you see is what you get'. And that is a major, if not *the* major, reason for her success.

Managing activities and resources checklist

If you feel under pressure, with too little time to manage too many activities, here are some issues to think about. You might want to find a few, valuable minutes to take a clean sheet of paper and jot down any ideas that the following list generates.

Work/life balance

Is your work and your time outside work in balance? Do you work long hours because you have to, or because you feel out of control? What steps could you take right now to redress the balance? Can you protect an evening each week for yourself? What is the equivalent of the 'Mum and Jo night' for you?

Passion

Are you passionate about what you do? Do you believe wholeheartedly in your organisation's products or services? If not, think about what is driving you to succeed throughout your working week. Give some thought to what you *are* passionate about. Is it time for a change?

Be yourself

Take a look in a mirror. Are you 'yourself' at work? Are you aware of consciously playing different roles to achieve certain outcomes? For example, do you find yourself enjoying playing the 'tough guy', even though it's not really you? Would your colleagues and staff say that they know you? How well? Are you open and transparent? What effect would it have if you made the decision to be yourself from now on?

People and culture

Do you cascade information quickly and effectively to your people? Are your people able to share their ideas and concerns with you? Are your people your greatest resource? Do you know your people, and do they know you? How would you describe the culture in your organisation? Are you proud of it? Is your organisation's culture holding you back, or driving you forward? What can you do about it? Are you and all your people working together towards a common goal?

Efficiency

What measures do you have in place to monitor the efficiency of your organisation? Would you know if a particular team or department was less efficient than others? What incentive do you have for introducing more efficient measures? Do you have an 'if it ain't broke, don't fix it' mentality? How often do you review how efficient your organisation is being?

Project schedules and delivery

As a manager or leader, do you demand that projects are delivered on time, to budget and to the standard required? Do you deliver that yourself? Do you plan the steps you or your people will take to deliver a project? How often do you review progress made on a project?

Finance

Can you currently measure the return on investment for every marketing pound that you or your organisation spends? Do you review the effectiveness of every flyer, every mailing, or every marketing activity that you undertake? What steps would you need to take in order to be able to do so? What is stopping you taking them? On balance, are you using your marketing budget effectively?

Priorities and deadlines

Is your agenda set for you, or do you set it yourself? What motivates you to get something done? If it isn't a matter of personal pride, then should it be? Do you work in a high-pressured environment? If you do, should you be doing so? Can you influence the environment in which you manage or lead? Do you often feel 'time-poor'? What steps could you take to win back some valuable time? Are you able to switch off?

National Occupational Standards

This book covers the NOS Management and Leadership standards
– Using Resources. The following table will help you to locate these
competencies in the book.

Competency	Unit no.	Chapter	Chapter title
Manage a budget	E1	2	How can you manage a budget and arrange finance?
Manage finance for your area of responsibility	E2	2	How can you manage a budget and arrange finance?
Obtain additional finance for the organisation	E3	2	How can you manage a budget and arrange finance?

Competency	Unit no.	Chapter	Chapter title
Promote the use of technology within your organisation	E4	3	How is technology best used and promoted?
Ensure your own actions reduce risk to health and safety	E5	4	How can you ensure health and safety requirements are met?
Ensure health and safety requirements are met in your area of responsibility	E6	4	How can you ensure health and safety requirements are met?
Ensure an effective organisational approach to health and safety	E7	4	How can you ensure health and safety requirements are met?
Manage physical resources	E8	5	How can you manage physical resources?
Manage the environmental impact of your work	E9	6	What impact on the environment does your work have?

Competency	Unit no.	Chapter	Chapter title
Take effective decisions	E10	7	How can you make the right decisions?
Communicate information and knowledge	E11	8	How can you manage knowledge and information?
Manage knowledge in your area of responsibility	E12	8	How can you manage knowledge and information?
Promote knowledge managements in your organisation	E13	8	How can you manage knowledge and information?
Support team and virtual working	E14	9	How can you support team working?
Procure supplies	E15	10	How can you find the right suppliers?
Select suppliers through a tendering process	E16	10	How can you find the right suppliers?
Outsource business processes	E17	11	When should you outsource parts of the business?

Further information and reading

Useful organisations and websites

Chartered Management Institute
Management House
Cottingham Road
Corby NN17 1TT
Tel: 01536 204222
For information about all aspects of management and management qualifications.

Management Standards Centre
3rd Floor, 2 Savoy Court
Strand
London WC2R 0EZ
Tel: 0207 240 2826
www.management-standards.org/home

Official UK Government website
www.direct.gov.uk
For a wide variety of information including employment and education.

Department for Business Innovations and Skills
Ministerial Correspondence Unit
1 Victoria St, London SW1H 0EY
Tel: 0207 215 5000
www.bis.gov.uk
For information about all aspects of business.

Learndirect
www.learndirect-business.com
For advice about all sorts of business training and courses.

Chambers of Commerce
www.chamberonline.co.uk
Local Chambers of Commerce are good sources of information on a variety of local and national business matters.

Business Link
Tel: 0845 600 9006
www.businesslink.gov.uk
Business Link is a government-funded network of local advice centres for business.

Mailing Preference Service
Mailing Preference Service
Freepost 29
LON 20771
London W1E 0ZT
Tel: 0845 7034599
www.mpsonline.org.uk
Registering with this service will reduce the amount of junk mail you receive.

Health & Safety Executive
HSE Information Services
Caerphilly Business Park
Caerphilly CF83 3GG
Infoline: 0845 345 0055

Chartered Institute of Water and Environmental Management (CIWEM)
www.ciwem.org

Chartered Institute of Environmental Health (CIEH)
www.cieh.org

Association of Noise Consultants
www.association-of-noise-consultants.co.uk

Energy Institute
www.energyinstitute.org

Environmental Data Services
www.ends.co.uk

Islamic Bank of Great Britain
www.islamic-bank.com

Intellectual Property Office
www.ipo.gov.uk

Useful reading

Baguley, Phil, *Leading People* (Hodder Education, Instant Manager) 2010

Bird, Polly, *Write the Perfect Business Plan* (Hodder Education, Teach Yourself) 2010

Callis, Sidney, *Working with People* (Hodder Education, Instant Manager) 2010

Peppit, Ed, *Six of the Best – lessons in life and leadership* (Hodder Arnold) 2007

HSE, Management of Health & Safety at Work (HSE) 2000

Ramsden, Philip, *Finance for Non-financial Managers* (Hodder Education, Teach Yourself) 2010

Walmsley, Bernice, *Getting Results* (Hodder Education, Instant Manager) 2009

Walmsley, Bernice, *Managing Change* (Hodder Education, Instant Manager) 2009

Walmsley, Bernice, *Managing Yourself* (Hodder Education, Instant Manager) 2010

Index